the Zinester's Guide to Portland

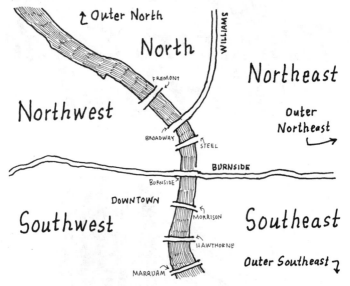

How to Use this Guide

We broke the Zinester's Guide to Portland into sections to make it easy to find what you need. There are separate sections for geographic areas of the city (NW, SW, etc.) and outer Portland areas (St. Johns, Roseway, etc.). You'll also find special sections for things like 'Bicycling in Portland', 'Bridges' and 'Museums'.

In each of the geographic sections you will find categories such as 'Restaurants', 'Theaters', and 'Parks'.

If you know the name of something specific, look for it in the Index at the back of the Guide.

Please remember that things change; use the phone numbers and/or websites provided to check that a business is still open or if the hours have changed. You can also check our website (pdxguide.org) for up-to-date information.

And just because a business is mentioned in the Guide, it doesn't mean that the authors are 100% behind it; ownership or quality of services can change at any time. Take all listings with a grain of salt and rely on your own judgement.

If you find errors or omissions, please contact us:

pdxguide.org ~ P. O. Box 14185, Portland, OR 97293-0185 ~ editor@pdxguide.org

Editor: Shawn Granton **Book Design, Cover, Webhead:** Nate Beaty

Written By: Nate Beaty (nb), Carye Bye (cb), Jessica Byers (jb), Joe Biel (job), Krissy Durden (kd), Nicole Georges (ng), Rebecca Gilbert (rg), Shawn Granton (sg), Scott Larkin (sl), Kate Lopresti (kl), Emily Nilsson (en), Nickey Robo (nr), RevPhil Sano (rs), Molly Springlmeyer (ms), Ian Stude (is), Jon Van Oast (jv)

Art By: Nik Arnold (na), Nate Beaty (nb), Elijah Brubaker (eb), Chris Cilla (cc), Ezra Claytan Daniels (ecd), Nicole Georges (ng), Shawn Granton (sg), Lydia Greer (lg), Uriah Herr (uh), Alicia Justus (aj), Chris Larson (cl), Chris Larson (cl), Alec Longstreth (al), Carolyn Main (cm), Seann McKeel (sm), Greg Means (gm), Dan Miller (dm), Jay Moreno (jm), Bruce Orr (bo), Heather Q (hq), Aaron Renier (ar), Androo Robinson (aro), Tim Root (tr), Khris Soden (ks), Eliza Starky (es), Dylan Williams (dw)

Introduction

Hello! Welcome to the Zinester's Guide to Portland. I'm Shawn, the editor of this here thing. Thanks for dropping by! You may ask yourself what exactly is the Zinester's Guide? Well, it's a travel resource initially designed for zinesters, the typically budgetary restricted connoisseurs and producers of underground literature. It was started way back in 2001 by a gaggle of such zine-type folk, created to be a complimentary guide for attendees of the first Portland Zine Symposium. Its beginnings were humble, a 16 page photocopied and folded pamphlet.

Now we're at the Fourth Edition, a massive 128 page book professionally printed with a fancy-ass cover by Nate Beaty. Whaddya think? (Save your comments for after reading it!) Big thanks to Joe Biel of Microcosm Publishing for taking up the reins of publishing this; my long-arm stapler was beginning to wear out from all the reprints we had to do of the Third Edition!

Inside you'll find hundreds of listings about many different things going on in the Rose City. We've broken it down by geographic "quadrant" to make it easy to find things, and from there each quadrant is broken into categories such as Record Stores, Restaurants, Parks, etc. The Zinester's Guide has never been strictly for zinesters. It has always been about sharing the interesting and unique things that make Stumptown great, and also helping people get by that aren't swimming in scads of money. Pretty much all the restaurants listed within are economical, and you'll be able to walk away spending less than $10 yet feel satisfied. (Oh yeah, all the restaurants listed are veggie friendly!)

We do this to share the special Portland that we know intimately. Portland is a subtle city, and its charms might not be apparent at first glance. We're not a humongous tourist destination, not as much as other cities of the West Coast. So we don't benefit from the big obvious touristy destinations of Seattle, San Francisco, or Los Angeles. But that doesn't mean that we are a boring town! You just have to look a little harder. And this guide is to help you find the things that interest you, so you don't feel so lost your first time here.

This isn't just a traveler's guide. We intend this to be of value to the resident of the Bridge City, whether you've lived here 3 months, 3 years, or all your life. If you haven't been hiding under a rock, you may have noticed that Portland has become a happening town. There are so many things going on in town that it's been hard to keep track of it all, myself included. We add new stuff to the Guide with every new edition, so maybe you'll find something in here that you hadn't heard about!

We realize that the Zinester's Guide to Portland isn't perfect. No guidebook is.

This book has been created by volunteers who don't always have lots of time to dedicate to this project. And Portland's a big town. Things are bound to slip through the cracks. We may have had to omit things because of lack of room or relevancy. Businesses close frequently, and quality of restaurants can go downhill in the course of a couple years, so just because its in here doesn't mean it's always going to be there or that it will be good. Please let us know if you notice any errors, business closures, or glaring omissions.

Or better yet, write for the Zinester's Guide! This is built with volunteer submissions and we make it easy to contribute. Either write us c/o the PO Box found in the title page or go to our website's online submission form at http://pdx-guide.org/submit/ You'll also be able to check out our ever-expanding online database of listings!

I'd like to thank each and every one of our contributors who provided writings, drawings, or both. You'll find their names listed on page three and their initials next to listings or drawings. If you would like to get in touch with anyone here, please write them care of us, and we'll pass along the info. Big thanks go to Nate Beaty, designer and web-dude of the Guide. Without him we wouldn't be reading this today.

And a very special thanks to YOU, dear reader of the Guide! We hope you get something out of our humble publication. Please let us know what you think.

And enjoy Portland!

Shawn Granton
"Editor"

A note about the illustrations found within:

You may notice that everything pictured in this guide is a hand-drawn illustration. Not many guides feature actual illustrations of places in the way we use them. Our artists spent a lot of time drawing these pieces.

If your business is one of those depicted in an illustration in the Zinester's Guide to Portland, please note that every illustration is copyrighted to their respective artist. If you would like to use that illustration, please contact us first. We'll put you in touch with the respective artist and they can give their approval. And hey, if you are a business, give the artist something for their work. It may not have to be actual money, it could just be free tickets to a movie, some coffee, a gift certificate, services that you offer, etc. In short, be nice about it and please don't just go ahead and use a drawing in here without checking first.

A Very Brief History of the City of Roses By Khris Soden

In 1841, near the beginning of the great overland migrations to the Oregon Terri-
tory, two men sharing a canoe ride from Fort Vancouver(in what is now Washington
State) to Oregon City stopped in a low clearing to rest during the course of the
afternoon. One of the men, William Overton, a drifter from Tennessee, stated that
the area was his land claim, and that if the other man, Asa Lovejoy, a lawyer from
Boston, would pay to file the land claim, Overton would give him half-ownership.
Lovejoy liked the location, and agreed to do it. Several months later, Overton
sold his half of the claim to Francis Pettygrove, a merchant from Maine, for fifty
dollars in supplies and then left the area, never to be heard from again. Lovejoy
and Pettygrove started clearing the trees in the area, platting roads, and laying
the groundwork for a new townsite. Unable to agree on a name for their future city
(they both wanted to name it after their home towns), they agreed to flip a coin on
it. Pettygrove won, and named the fledgling town site Portland in honor of Portland,
Maine.

In 1851, when the settlement had grown to a population of 850, Portland was
officially incorporated as a city. During this time period, Portland enjoyed consider-
able economic growth as the Northwest's only shipping port (Seattle had yet to be
founded), and was doing brisk business with San Francisco, thanks to California's
gold rush. Sea trade was also being done with the East Coast, the Sandwich
Islands (now Hawaii), and China. This trade, along with the eventual depletion of
gold in California, brought an influx of immigrants to Portland, and the city had
grown to a population of 70,000 by the beginning of the 1880's.

Like all cities, Portland was developing its own personality, and in the case of the
City of Roses, it was a split personality. On its most public face, Portland is a gen-
tile, blue-blooded community; on the other side was the Mr. Hyde: a city of racism,
vice and corruption. This was perhaps most evident in the 1880's, a time when
Portland was investing in education and city parks, but also gaining a reputation
for being the "roughest seaport in the World". Portland had purchased the first city
block for the Park Blocks in 1867 and in the 1880's had acquired City Park (now
Washington Park). Public schools had been in place for nearly twenty years, and
a public library was in the works. Steven Skidmore bequeathed a public fountain
to be built in the commercial center of the city. Also during this period, there was
a backlash against the Chinese population, which comprised nearly a third of the
city's citizens. Riots against the Chinese led to an exodus of sorts, with many of
them returning to China, or relocating to San Francisco. The need for able-bodied
seamen prompted the practice of 'shanghai-ing': kidnapping men, then selling
them to unscrupulous captains in need of crew. The North End (now known as Old
Town/Chinatown) was a haven for prostitution and drugs, much as it is to-day.

Corruption on the police force was rampant, and the entire force was replaced twice during the 1880's.

By the turn of the century, Portland had attained the status of a small metropolis, and to prove it, in 1905, they hosted a World's Fair-style Lewis and Clark Centennial Exposition. Built around the now-filled-in Guilds Lake in Northwest Portland, the Exposition featured cultures from around the world, extravagant electric lighting, and the world's largest log cabin (which later housed the World Forestry Center, until the structure burned down in 1964). Over one million people visited the Exposition during the summer that it existed, and many moved to Portland afterwards; by the 1920's, Portland's population exceeded 250,000 people. The early part of the century also brought progressive politics and city-planning to the city's government.

During World War II, Portland played an important role in the war effort by being one of the primary centers for ship-building. By the end of the war, roughly 150,000 people were employed by the shipyards. A large percentage of the shipyard employees were African-Americans who had come from the East for work. Predominantly white Portland showed it's racist stripes when mortgage insurance companies "red-lined" black neighborhoods to imply they were bad risk neighborhoods; in 1950, an anti-discrimination ordinance was defeated in the general election.

Through the late 1950's and 1960's, Portland embarked on ambitious series of "urban renewal" projects, the first (and probably the most devastating) being the South Auditorium Urban Renewal Project, which almost entirely erased South Portland, displacing thousands of the city's Jewish and Italian families. The Stadium Freeway project destroyed 14 city blocks of downtown, and the Fremont Bridge sliced through Albina. The Morrison Bridge eradicated seven blocks of downtown's original Chinatown.

Although the city had done a good deal of damage to it's cultural and social aspects during the middle of the twentieth century, the 1970's saw the beginning of a new era for Portland, when the city began to refocus on neighborhoods, parks, and public transportation. A plan to cut a wide freeway (termed the "Mount Hood Freeway") through the middle of Southeast Portland was scrapped, and on the edge of the Willamette, Waterfront Park was created out of a cleared highway (Harbor Drive). In 1979, the Urban Growth Boundary was established to combat the sprawl that has affected other Western cities. Light rail (MAX) came to the city in 1986.

Today, Portland likes to endorse its livability and the "creative class" of citizens, such as artists, musicians, and designers. Unfortunately, an aspect of promoting these is the gentrification of older neighborhoods, and higher rental rates. The city has become more careful about preserving its historic past and architecture, but sometimes still turns a blind eye to "developing" neighborhoods.

It's a great city to ride a bike in. At least, if you don't mind a little rain.

Getting Around Town
By Kate Lopresti

If you have no intention of driving out to the Oregon coast (90 miles) or heading to the Pendleton Round-Up (200 miles), there's no need to have a car while you visit Portland. There are better ways to get around that cost you less and allow you to see more.

Walking is recommended when you travel short distances and want to explore individual neighborhoods. Biking is king if the weather is good and, of course, you have a bike to ride while you're here. Finally, there is Portland's public transit system, which is impressive for a town this size.

Of the 93 routes that make up Portland's transit system, 16 of them run every fifteen minutes or more, even on Sundays. Every route has wheelchair and bike access. What's more, you can ride in certain areas for free. Tell *that* to your hometown bus company.

Route and Schedules

For help finding your stop and planning your trip, you can call 503-238-RIDE (7499) or visit www.trimet.org. TriMet, the city's transit company, also has a service counter in the Visitor Information building at Pioneer Courthouse Square. There you can ask questions, buy tickets, and collect the schedules of all the routes. The service counter is open Monday through Friday 8:30 a.m. to 5:00 p.m. On Saturdays the building is open from 10:00 a.m. to 4 p.m. This gives you access to the "Trip Center," where you can buy tickets or use the trip planning kiosk.

Fares

The city is divided into three zones and where you travel between them determines the cost of your fare. Most trips within Portland will cost you $1.70 (the 1 and 2 zone fare). A trip from Portland to a suburb—Beaverton, Gresham, Hillsboro, Milwaukie—is usually a three zone fare ($2.00). Fares are the same for the bus, light rail, and streetcar.

The Transfer

After you pay your fare on the bus, the driver will hand you a transfer. Don't lose it! Not only is this your receipt, it is also your ticket to ride until the hour printed at the top. Usually you have 60 minutes to ride on weekdays and 2 hours to ride on weekends; however, sometimes drivers don't always rip the transfers off the dispenser just so. Instead, probably to save time, they take a stack marked for 2 or 3 hours ahead and hand them out until the end of the route. 3 hours of riding the bus? You should be so lucky!

Transit Mall

Downtown Portland is home to the Transit Mall on SW 5th and 6th avenues. Here you can pick up any number of buses that run throughout the city. Bus stops run up and down both streets and are grouped by the areas of the city the buses serve. On 5th Avenue you will find stops for buses headed into southeast, south, southwest, and west Portland. The stops on 6th Avenue are for routes to north, northeast, and Union Station.

Buses

At the front of each bus is the line number and name. Buses that go to Portland's city center read "To Portland." Many buses have one number, but two routes. For example, the eastside's 15 Belmont becomes 15 NW 23rd Avenue after it crosses the Morrison bridge and enters downtown. The 4 Division becomes the 4 Fessenden when it runs from southeast Portland to north Portland. Check the number and the name of your bus before boarding.

The Metropolitan Area Express (MAX)

MAX is Portland's light rail system and it offers three lines: the Red line takes you from Beaverton Transit Center through downtown and on to the Portland International Airport (PDX); the Blue line runs from the westside suburb of Hillsboro through downtown and out to Gresham. The newest line in the mix, the Yellow line, runs from the Rose Quarter north to the Expo Center.

The MAX is an excellent way to get to the outskirts of town and into the suburbs without the frequent stops that buses usually make in inner Portland. If for some reason you need to run out to Beaverton's Costco for an economy size box of Hot Pockets, MAX is your best bet.

You can use your bus transfer as proof of payment on MAX. There are also ticket machines at every stop. Keep your ticket or transfer handy as fare inspectors frequently hop on board looking for freeloaders.

Portland Streetcar

The streetcar runs from Portland State University to Good Samaritan Hospital on Northwest 23rd Avenue. Your bus transfer or MAX ticket is valid on the streetcar. Also, there is a ticket machine on board.

The MAX! (nb)

All-Day Ticket

If you expect to be riding around a lot while you are in town, consider TriMet's All-Day ticket ($4.25) or the 7 Day Pass ($16.50 for two zones, $19.50 for all zones). This gives you unlimited riding on the bus, MAX, and streetcar for one day or seven days, respectively.   All day passes can be purchased on any bus or MAX staion, while 7 Day Passes are available from the TriMet Service Counter at Pioneer Courthouse Square or at some area Safeway and Fred Meyer stores.

Fareless Square

Not really a square, this area in and around downtown Portland is where you ride free all day, every day. Trimet.org describes Fareless Square as the downtown area "within the boundaries of the Willamette River, NW Irving Street, and the I-405 freeway, as well as MAX stations from the Rose Quarter to Lloyd Center and bus stops along NE Multnomah to 13th Avenue."

On a map, this makes perfect sense. In practice, you need something more concrete. Think of it this way: When you get off the Greyhound in downtown Portland you can hop a bus—say, "Fareless, please," to the driver—and ride as far south as Portland State University FOR FREE! Or, if you're hanging out at Central Library, reading People magazine on the cheap, you can then board the MAX and ride all the way to Lloyd Center Mall on the other side of the river FREE! Or maybe you're hanging out at the Portland Art Museum and you decide you need some book learning, hop on the streetcar behind the museum and take it straight to Reading Frenzy without spending a dime.

Questions?

If you're not sure if the bus stopped in front of you is the one you want or you need help finding your stop, don't be afraid to ask bus drivers for help. They know routes like zinesters know postal rates. (kl)

Hey, maybe you aren't currently in Portland, and would like to know how to get here! Here are some options:

Trimet! (nb)

Getting To and From Portland

VIA TRAIN

Amtrak offers a number of train lines into the Rose City.

Coast Starlight—this train runs daily between Los Angeles and Seattle, connecting us with the San Francisco Bay Area, and Eugene to the south, Tacoma and Olympia to the north. The Starlight has quite a reputation, partially due to the natural beauty along the route, partially due to its chronic latenes. If you use the Star-Late, expect delays of several hours coming from the south.

Empire Builder—this train runs daily between Portland and Chicago, connecting us with Spokane, Minneapolis and Milwaukee, to the east. This route can also be quite scenic, especially going through the Columbia River Gorge and the Rocky Mountains/Glacier National Park.

Cascades—these are European designed Talgo trains unique to North America. There are three daily trips north to Seattle, and two daily trips south to Eugene. For an additional fee ($5) you can bring along your bicycle without boxing it.

Portland's Union Station *(800 NW Sixth Ave, cross street Irving)* is conveniently located at the north end of the Transit Mall downtown. (You can't miss the station; it's got a tower that says, "Go by Train!")

For Amtrak info, call 1-800-USA-RAIL or go to www.amtrak.com

If you're coming from Vancouver, B.C. or other Canadian points, there is one daily Cascades train (plus several busses) connecting Vancouver's Pacific Central Station to Seattle's King St. Station. For more info regarding rail travel in Canada, call Via Rail Canada at 1-888-VIA-RAIL or go to www.viarail.ca

VIA BUS

The Greyhound station is located at 550 NW 6th Ave, conveniently one block south of Union Station. You know what you get with Greyhound, so no need to elaborate here, but we will add that Greyhound has cut many services to the smaller towns in Oregon and Washington, making it less useful. For Greyhound info, call 1 (800) 229-9424 or go to www.greyhound.com

Additionally, there are Amtrak Thruway bus service that serves many destinations within the state. Buses depart from the front of Union Station. For info, ask at the station or call 800-USA-RAIL

VIA AIR

Portland International Airport is located at 7000 NE Airport Way (503-460-4234) which is on the outskirts of town. To get from there to downtown, you can a) hail a cab and pay upwards of $20 (plus tip), or b) take the new Airport MAX, which is inexpensive ($1.70), runs frequently, and takes about 20 minutes to get to downtown.

HITCHIN'/RIDESHARE

There are plenty of off-ramps to stick a thumb out along the freeways of Portland. Of course, it's all illegal.

If you are looking for more of a formal rideshare, check out Craigslist, under Rideshare: portland.craigslist.com/rid/ There is also rideshare info posted at Portland's two hostels, see their listings under hostels.

VIA CAR

The primary north-south artery in and out of Portland is Interstate-5 (I-5). This superhighway (or, if you will, "freeway") goes from the Canadian border to the Mexican border, slicing through Seattle, Eugene, Sacramento, Los Angeles, and San Diego. If you're coming from the bay area, take I-80 east, where you'll connect with I-5 in Sact-o. If you're coming from any of California's spectacular and numerous cities of the Central Valley (Fresno, Modesto, Bakersfield, etc) you can take California Highway 99 north to Sacramento and connect with I-5 there. An alternate route from the south is US Route 101, which connects to Los Angeles and San Francisco, but closer to the coast than I-5. From San Fran, US-101 crosses the Golden Gate Bridge (oooh! aahhh!) and hugs the Pacific for most of the many miles to Astoria, passing through Eureka/Arcata, Coos Bay, Newport, and the coast redwood forests! It's a slower, more meandering route than straight-shot I-5, but if you have the time, it just might be worth it. To get to Portland from US-101, you can take Oregon Highway 6 east from Tillamook and then connect to US-26 (the Sunset Highway) which will bring you into Portland. From the east, Interstate 84 (I-84) connects Portland to Salt Lake City, passing through high desert metropoli like Pendleton, La Grande, and Boise. This is probably your best route from most of the Great Basin or the Central Rockies utilizing connections to I-80 and I-15 in Salt Lake City. If you're coming from central/eastern Washington State, Northern Rockies, or Montana, take either I-90 west or US-2 west into Spokane and then take US-395 south to the sprawling Tri-Cities. Then take I-82 east, crossing the Columbia, connecting with I-84 just west of Pendleton.

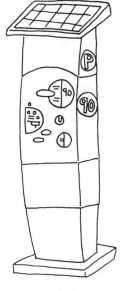

(gm)

The "Official" PDX Neighborhood Guide

The city of Portland is divided into five sectors: Southeast, Northeast, South-west, Northwest, and North. Burnside Street is the divider of north from south (addresses on Burnside are either W or E), and the Willamette River divides east from west. When the city planners were devising this "quadrant" system of compartmentalizing Portland way back in 1931 they noted that the Willamette makes a 45° turn just north of the Burnside Bridge. This would mean that some points in the Northeast would be further west than some points in the Northwest! The compromise solution to correct this was to create a just plain ol' "North" quadrant, divided from the Northeast by Williams Avenue.

All addresses in the City of Portland contain the respective sector it's located in, noted by the abbreviations SE, NE, SW, NE, and N (for example, 2026 NE Alberta St.) For most purposes, when people are asked where they live, they refer to their sector (for example, "I live in the Southeast", or "I live in North Portland") In each of these sectors; there are a multitude of unique neighborhoods. Here we'll give you a brief rundown of the major ones that are closest to the city center, so you'll be able to explore the city more effectively

Northwest

The Northwest is an interesting area. While it's the most urbanized area of the city (and the state), and the most gentrified (or yuppified) part. There is still bits of the ol' grit to be found, but they're few and far between.

The Northwest Hills is the general term for the north-of-Burnside neighborhoods that straddle the Tualatin Mountains. Here you'll find some great views of the city (especially at Pittock Mansion), and some really nice homes. Downhill, you'll find the "heart" of this sector, the boringly named "Northwest Neighbor-hood" (some of the more "sophisticated" residents like to refer to it as "Nob Hill"). This neighborhood is bounded by W Burnside, I-405, the Willamette, NW Nicolai, and the Hills. Up until the 1990's, this area was fairly sketchy and run down (the movie "Drugstore Cowboy" was shot here). Then the developers had their way with it. They converted it all into upscale "condos" and boutiques, and now the SUV-to-cellphone ratio is quite high.

The dual business axis of this area is NW 21st and NW 23rd Aves.

Twenty-Third (sometimes derisively referred to as "Trendy-Third") is a yuppie's wet dream. All sorts of corporate chain stores can be found here (Pottery Barn, Urban Outfitters, etc), plus way-overpriced, wait-two-hours-to-be-seated type restaurants, and two Starbucks. Budget-busting. There are e a couple of cool things here, but sometimes dealing with the "Twenty Third Attitude" isn't worth it. Twenty-First is more laid back, more bar-and-food and less "boutique". But the frat mentality here is quite high on the weekends, and there's also a Starbucks here.

Further east is the Pearl District (bounded by I-405, W Burnside, NW Broadway, and the river). Until the mid-1990's, this was a forgotten warehouse-and-industrial district, with its streets criss-crossed by railroad tracks. Then, like Northwest, the Pearl was "discovered". (The moniker "Pearl District" didn't happen until the gentrification started, previously it was known as the North-west Industrial District.) Now many of the warehouses are filled with lofts and art galleries. The city would like to think this is the artistic heart of the city, but it's a "heart" wrapped up in Benjamins.

And if you go even further east, you'll find Old Town (bounded by NW Broadway, W Burnside, and the river). This is historically Portland's "Skid Row" (along with the Skidmore Historic District just to its south). For now, the area still retains much of its grit, filled with nightclubs (of the shitty type) and crack hotels, but there are signs that things are changing, with new art galleries sprouting up here and there. Within Old Town, you'll find our postage-stamp sized Chinatown.

Southwest

In the southwest, you'll find Downtown, which is pretty self-explanatory (y'know, tall buildings, businesspeople, offices, city government, stores, and the like). Radiating southwestward from there is the Southwest Hills. Here you'll find some splendiferous parks like Washington Park and Council Crest, awesome views, narrow, windy roads, and tons of spendy houses.

South of downtown between the river and the hills is the neighborhoods of Lair Hill and Corbett-Terwilliger. This area is the remaining vestige of South Portland, a predominantly Jewish and Italian neighborhood that was leveled in the early '60s in the city's misguided "urban renewal" attempts. What's left are some cool houses and views of the Willamette. though the concentration of so many major traffic arteries (I-5, Barbur Blvd, Front Ave, Macadam Ave, the Ross Island Bridge Ramps) in such a narrow area gives the neighborhood a very cut-off and claustrophobic feel. You can't go more than two blocks without having to figure out how to negotiate around an on-ramp or freeway.

Beyond all that, the Southwest is a mystery zone of hills, strip malls, major streets, and general suburbia. Unfortunately, we don't really know much about what goes on here. There are a handful of things worth checking out if you really had the time, like Multnomah Village and some nice parks (Tryon Creek, Gabriel), but if you don't have the time, don't worry too much about missing it.

Southeast

The East Side of the Willamette River is "where it's at" in this town. Most of Portland's population lives over here, including most every zinester. Southeast used to be somewhat sketchy ten to twenty years ago (34th and Belmont used to be heroin central), but most of that feel has been long gone.

The first neighborhood in the southeast coming from downtown is Buckman (bounded by the river, E Burnside, SE 28th, and SE Hawthorne). The western part of Buckman (up to SE 12th) is also referred to as the Central Eastside Industrial District. Lots of warehouses abound here; some of which have been taken over by artists. Cheap-ish loftspace can still be found here, though the developers are making their first stabs in the 'hood. Also adding to the area's cool is Lower Burnside (or if you are really that type of person who feels the need to throw around oh-so-hip names for neighborhoods in the vein of SoHo, LoBu) the new nightlife district lining E Burnside from the bridge to 12th. What was once an area for used cars, sketchy motels, and street deals now includes "the hippest club in Portland" (Doug Fir) and "Portland's Rock and Roll Motel" (Jupiter Motel). What will be next?

East of Buckman is Sunnyside (bounded by SE 28, SE Stark, SE 49th, and SE Hawthorne), originally a "streetcar suburb". Sunnyside is the most "happening" neighborhood in Southeast, containing both the Belmont and Hawthorne commercial districts. This is the area that many new residents of Portland desire to move to (I can attest to that), but the rents in the area can be a bit pricey.

The commercial district known as Hawthorne extends primarily from SE 30th and SE 42nd Aves along Hawthorne Blvd (although stuff can be found as far west as SE 11th and as far east as SE 52nd). This was once a run-down commercial strip, but it has seen quite a transformation over the last decade or so. Now it's the "bohemian" district of PDX. When most mainstream guidebooks get around to talking about the eastside, Hawthorne is usually the only thing mentioned, usually adding adjectives as "quirky" and the ever-stupid "funky". Expect several shops to buy neat gift ideas, cheap eats, head shops, cool record and book stores, street musicians, hippies, spangers, and relentless petitioners.

Belmont is Hawthorne's younger cousin, six blocks north of its relative. Centered on SE 34th and SE Belmont, there's a plethora of good eateries, coffee shops, and markets in a very small area.

Going eastward is the Mount Tabor neighborhood, centered around its name-sake volcano. South is the Richmond neighborhood (does every town have its own Richmond neighborhood?) bounded by SE 30th, SE Hawthorne, SE 50th, and SE Powell). It's mostly residential here as well. And for some reason, the majority of Portland's hippies seem to live here.

South of the Buckman is Hosford-Abernathy (bounded by the river, SE Hawthorne, SE 30th, and SE Powell). The two things H-A is most known for is Ladd's Addition and the Clinton St. commercial district. Ladd's Addition is bound by SE Hawthorne, SE 12th, SE 20th, and SE Division. Ladds is unique because its streets are laid out in a radial "X" pattern (rather than the grid that the rest of PDX is based on). William Sargent Ladd, a prominent businessman and mayor, subdivided what was his 126-acre farm here in 1891. Inspired by Pierre L'Enfant's plan for Washington, D.C., Ladd designed the plat based on a diagonal street system surrounding a central park (Ladd's Circle). Also included are four diamond-shaped parks, located where some of the diagonal streets meet. Stroll through Ladd's and peep the cool turn-of-the-century arts-and-crafts houses, rose gardens, and stately Dutch Elms that line the streets. The Clinton St. District is centered on SE 26th and SE Clinton, and only extends one block in each direction. But within this one block radius is two good record shops, an arthouse theatre, a wicked video store, and good food! Head two blocks north to Division St. and find more stuff to do, though it's more spread out (between SE 20th and SE 50th).

Northeast

The Northeast is an interesting mix of different, contrasting neighborhoods. Generally speaking, this area, along with North Portland, is where the cheapest housing can be found within the central city, which is why you'll find a lot of punk rock types here. Northeast and North contain what some would consider "bad areas", though a lot of that assumption has to do with poor knowledge of the area, mixed with a dash of racism. Conversely, Northeast has some affluent areas as well, sometimes butted up against the poorer areas.

The first neighborhood from downtown via the Burnside Bridge is the Kerns, bounded by the river, I-84, NE 32nd, and E Burnside. Probably due to the proximity of both Sandy and I-84, Kerns is lousy with apartment complexes, sometimes cool Southern-California-Spanish-Mission-Courtyard style from back in the 20's and 30's, sometimes ugly 70's shitboxes. In Kerns, a commercial strip has revived along E 28th Ave. between NE Glisan and SE Ankeny. This area was a "red-light" district up until the new century, but has seen an extensive clean-up in that time. Here you'll find not one, not two, but three wine bars, and many gourmet eateries. While much of it can be gross in the NW 23rd type of way, there's some cool things here, plus a bit of the ol' grime hasn't gone away, much to the dismay of the SUV set.

Eastward is Laurelhurst (bounded by NE 32nd, I-84, NE 45th, and SE Stark), also a "streetcar suburb". The streets here follow a weird pattern meandering around the hill rather than follow a grid. Laurelhurst was owned by W.S. Ladd, and as with other Ladd properties turned into neighborhoods (Ladd's Addition, Eastmoreland), the area is particularly well-off. In the middle is Coe Circle, where NE 39th meets NE Glisan. Check out the gold-leaf statue of Joan of Arc there.

Going north of I-84 closest to the river is the Lloyd District (bounded by the river, I-84, NE Broadway, and NE 16th). This area is the brainchild of a California oil millionaire, who started buying up the land in the 40's in order to create an auto-friendly "second downtown" to compete with the first. With its all-too-easy access to the Banfield Expressway (I-84), it became the home to Oregon's first enclosed shopping mall, the Lloyd Center. Surrounding it are tall office complexes isolated in a sea of parking lots. Well, it was someone's idea of progress, wasn't it?

To the north and east of Lloyd, you'll find Northeast's "money belt". Here's a series of neighborhoods (almost exclusively residential) that are full of spendy, "nice" houses. From west to east, they are Irvington, Alameda, Grant Park, and Beaumont-Wilshire. Through the "money belt" runs the Alameda Ridge, the only significantly steep hill in this part of town. Occasionally, there are some nice views of the city along it, but gargantuan houses have blocked out most of the overlooks. Also along the ridge are secret public stairways leading to the streets below (keep your eyes peeled for them!) Also in the area is NE Klickitat Street, famed residence of Beverly Cleary's Ramona the Brave (check out here statue in Grant Park!)

Eastward along infamous Sandy Blvd is Hollywood (bounded by NE 37th, NE Thompson, NE 47th, and I-84) This was Portland's first "second downtown" (does that make any sense?), a commercial hub far enough from downtown providing services for those who didn't want to travel all the way to the city center. Much of this district was built in the 1920's, during the time when streetcars were still dominant but the automobile was coming on strong. Hollywood's sleepy feel has persevered throughout the ages, as suburbia expanded further out and new auto-dependent shopping centers stole Hollywood's thunder. Because of that, you'll find some stuff you won't find elsewhere, like a couple old-school Chinese restaurants, a soda fountain, and one of the greatest cinemas in the Northwest. Surrounding Hollywood is Rose City Park, an area containing the city's largest collection of bungalow-style houses.

Heading north is where the current "action" of the Northeast is. North of NE Fremont St, you'll find the neighborhoods of King, Sabin, Vernon, and Concordia. One of the city's African-American areas, these neighborhoods have seen an influx of new ethnic groups into the area. Most conspicuous is the infusion of white twenty-somethings, attracted by the cheaper rents. Gentrification has been a hot topic as new blood displaces older residents and 'hood stalwarts slowly close. The traditional commercial artery is NE Martin Luther King Blvd, running northward through King, which is also seeing a bit of "urban renewal" these days.

The newer commercial strip of this area is Alberta Street (or if you prefer "Alberta Arts District") which is the barometer of what's occurring here. The District runs along Alberta St approximately between NE 12th and NE 31st Aves, cutting through most of the above-mentioned neighborhoods. Once a decimated light-industrial and commercial zone, now art galleries, restaurants, coffee shops, boutiques, and the like occupy the once-vacant storefronts, sitting alongside the auto-body, plumbing, and machinery shops that was once the backbone of the area. The art here is typically more organic than the stuff found in the Pearl. Alberta hosts the "Last Thursday Artwalk", where all galleries are open to the public. During the nicer months, Last Thursday becomes quite the spectacle, packed all the way up-and-down with people displaying their wares on the street, random street theater (especially at the Clown House at NE 25th), and tons and tons of people, making it one of the best free things to do in town.

North

The North "quadrant" is sort of the "secret" part of inner Portland. While not far from downtown, or particularly that hard to get to, it's still enough off the beaten path for most casual visitors to the city. (I doubt you'd find any listings for places to go in North Portland from a more traditional guidebook!) Also, for many years, the North has been considered an undesirable area by a lot of people outside of it (and still is today). That's a shame, because the North is as vital as any other sector of the city, and there are definitely things to do and see here.

Just to note: most people simply refer to this sector as "North Portland", rather than "the North". Some people call it NoPo, but the real hip kids refer to it as "the Peninsula", since both the Willamette and Columbia rivers form boundaries.

The closest neighborhoods to downtown are Boise and Eliot (collectively bound by the river, N/NE Broadway, NE MLK/7th, NE Skidmore, I-405, and I-5). These districts are also the heart of Albina. Since after World War II, Albina is the heart of African-American Portland. Because of that, Albina used to be synonymous with "ghetto" and "the wrong side of the tracks" for several decades. Albina was a city of its own for several decades of the nineteenth century, but it was consolidated with Portland (the original city on the westside of the Willamette) and East Portland (Albina's east bank neighbor to the south) in the 1890's. Because minorities have been the majority here since after the late 1940's, a lot of "urban renewal" projects have occurred here.

Boise/Eliot is a still lively, however. It's a commercial/industrial mix centered along the Mississippi and Vancouver/Williams corridors. The rest is filled with houses; many built during the last decades of the 19th century and the first decades of the 20th. Just like in the Northeast, there has been a recent influx of new people in the neighborhood. Much revitalization has been happening on Mississippi Avenue between N Fremont and N Skidmore. The development here is growing at an exponential rate, and many of the new businesses here don't mesh well with the neighborhood of old. Gentrification has become a major issue on the street, so much so that many people are not comfortable going on the street anymore.

Heading westward is Overlook, which straddles the bluff "overlooking" the Willamette. In this primarily residential area there are plenty of great views of the city and the West Hills to be found here, some of which are a bit "secret" (so get exploring!) N Interstate Ave is the primary north/south artery here, with businesses lining both sides of the street. Tri-Met opened the latest MAX light-rail line here (the Yellow, or Interstate line) in 2004. Make sure you check out the classic neon signs on the motels along the strip while you're there! Going deeper into the peninsula, you'll encounter several residential neighborhoods like Humboldt, Arbor Ridge, University Park, and Portsmouth. North of Ainsworth St between I-5 and MLK is Piedmont, a sleepy zone filled with shady, tree-lined streets and gorgeous old homes.

Outer Neighborhoods

Sellwood-Moreland, or more popularly just Sellwood is the last neighborhood along the eastbank of the Willamette River before the city of Milwaukie. Sellwood is one of Portland's most distinct neighborhoods partially due to its distance from down, and also because like St Johns to the north, it was once a separate city. The neighborhood is also unique in that it has two separate commercial axis, one centered at SE Milwaukie Av and Bybee Blvd, and one centered at SE 13th Av and Tacoma St. While both areas have become somewhat yuppified, Milwaukie/Bybee stays truer to its roots as the neighborhood "downtown", containing the services the area needs (grocery store, hardware store, banks, post office). 13th/Tacoma has become Portland's "Antique Row" and assumed the attitude suited to such a district.

Sellwood is a pretty quiet neighborhood, filled with nice houses and big trees. The riverside has been maintained in its natural state for the most part, providing great opportunities to see nature in the city. The bluff above the river bottoms provide choice views of the city, most notably along Sellwood Blvd and behind Llewellyn School.

Kenton is located in North Portland above Lombard St, west of I-5 and east of Chautauqua. Kenton was started as a company town for the meatpacking industry located along the Columbia River and Columbia Slough in the early 1900's. The company ran a streetcar line from the neighborhood down to the waterfront and built many a workers' house. It contains an old "downtown" along N Denver Ave where it meets N Interstate. Many of the buildings here are built with cinderblock, a rare sight in this city.

It looks like Kenton is waking from a long slumber. The opening of I-5 in the mid-sixties killed the commercial strip, and the moving of the meatpacking industry to other areas took many jobs out of the 'hood. Storefronts remained vacant for years. All that is changing since the Interstate (Yellow Line) MAX opened in May 2004, giving the district a quick, efficient connection to the rest of the city. Now the question is will gentrification occur? It's quite possible since N Mississippi will soon reach a saturation point. But in the meantime make sure you check out the Paul Bunyan statue at the intersection of N Interstate and N Denver!

At the tip of the Peninsula in North Portland you'll find St. Johns (no apostrophe needed!) St. Johns was once a city of its own, competing for predominance over the Willamette with Portland. It's distance from downtown saved it from annexation for awhile, but it eventually succumbed to the ever-expanding City of Roses in 1915. St. Johns retains its sense of "otherness", at once feeling like its own town, yet still part of Portland as a whole. The residents of the neighborhood are a proud bunch and have been resistant to change (especially in regards to bicycle facilities), though the hard exterior is chipping away as new blood infuses the neighborhood.

The "downtown" of St. Johns is located along N Lombard where it intersects with N Philadelphia. The area exudes a small town charm, almost like it hasn't waken up since the 1950's. St. Johns contains a healthy ethnic mix not commonly found elsewhere in the city. Many folks wonder if this area will ever be "discovered" (and subsequently gentrified), but its isolation from the rest of the city and the loyalty to the community from its residents runs deep, which may make it less than an ideal area to exploit in the eyes of a developer.

North

Art Supplies

S.C.R.A.P *3901-A N Williams Ave /
503-294-0769 / We-Sa 12p-6p, Su 12p-5*
SCRAP is an acronym of "The School and
Community Reuse Action Project". They
collect reusable items from businesses and
donations and distribute them to educators,
artists, families and kids for low-to-no
cost. SCRAP is an awesome place to find
neat supplies for all sorts of projects. The
inventory is constantly changing. You might
find fabric, paper, wire, tile, sticker vinyl,
office supplies or any other miscellaneous
treasures. They also host workshops and
have an area set aside for workspace for people to create in shop. Big bonus for the
friendly knowledgeable staff! And there are volunteer opportunities if you are interested.

(bo)

Bars

Albina Green *5128 N Albina Ave / 503-546-3183 / 3p - 10p* The replacement for the
Small World Café inside Big City Produce. Small, full-service bar with reasonably-priced
eatables. (nb)

Paragon Club *815 N Killingsworth St / 503-289-0888 / 10a-2:30a daily* Since the
previous Dingy North Portland Bar of Choice, The Jockey Club, was transformed into a
patch of grass, The Paragon has taken the title. Known for a rough-and-tussle mixed
crowd, it evens sports a buzz-in entry. Karaoke on Wed, Fri and Sat after 10. (nb)

Books, Zines, Comix and the like

Bridge City Comics *3725 N. Mississippi Ave / 503-282-5484 / 1am - 7pm Tuesday
through Saturday, 12pm - 5pm Sunday, Closed Mondays* Sparse and gallery-like comic
shop with equal parts mainstream and alternative, used and new. Friendly folks at the
counter. Located in the heart of the recently exploded Mississippi district. Sponsors a
Graphic Novel Reading Club for adults. (nb)

Coffeehouses, Teahouses and the like

Anna Bannanas (St Johns) *8716 N Lombard St / 503-286-2030 / Mo-Th 6:30a-
10p, Fr 6:30a-11p, Sa 8a-11p, Su 8a-9p*

James John Café *8527 N Lombard St / 503-285-4930* I've always imagined what it
would be like to live in St. Johns, the far-flung Peninsula neighborhood that feels like its

own city. One thing that's prevented me from moving there is the lack of decent coffee shops. Up until now. With the addition of an Anna Bannanas location just down the street, the James John Café ushers in the era of good coffee up there. (Unless you were satisfied with Starbucks, which means this may not be the right guidebook for you!) Serving the Stumptown and fresh baked pastries, the James John (not to be confused with the John St. Café) recently replaced a church-run cafe operated. And from inside you can look across Lombard and see the crown jewel of the 'hood – Thee St. Johns Bridge! The space (and menu) is a bit sparse right now, but expect a lunch and dinner menu soon. James John would be proud. (sg)

Muddy's Coffeehouse   *3560 N Mississippi Av / 503-445-6690 / Tu-Sa 7a-10p, Su 7a-6p* This café occupies the space of the former Purple Parlour. The charm of the Parlour remains, but the menu has been updated (sorry, it's no longer strictly vegetarian!) Muddy's serves up some decent breakfast and lunch, plus there's always a smattering of interesting daily specials. And can we say quiche? (sg)

The Waypost   *3120 N Williams Ave / 503-367-3182 / Mo 8a-4p, Tu-Fr 8a-10p, Sa 9a-10p, Su 9a-4p* A warm and unpretentious café, a good antidote to what is happening blocks away on Mississippi Ave. Great coffee (Stumptown), sweet vegan baked goods (which are still delicious as day-olds), and a hearty but limited food menu. The Waypost's main asset is its regular series of "lectures" and movie screenings, an information exchange based on a monthly topic. For example, the theme for March 2007 is philosophy and government. Folks are encouraged to get in touch with the Waypost to host a talk, and they don't even have to be an expert on the subject. (sg)

Chain Grocery Stores, Supermarkets, etc.

Fred Meyer (Interstate)   *7404 N Interstate Av / 503-286-6751 / 7a-11p daily*

New Seasons (Interstate)   *6400 N. Interstate Ave. / 503-467-4777*

Parks

Kelley Point Park   *all the way at the north-western most point of N Marine Drive, where it meets N Lombard* Sometimes failure is good. Back in the 1840's, when there were several towns along the Willamette vying to be "the city" of the Northwest, New Englander Hall J. Kelley attempted to build "the Manhattan of the Northwest" at what is now this park. It looks so logical when you view a map, since this is where the Willamette meets the Columbia. But the reality of trying to build a town on low, swampy land prone to flooding proved too much for even the hardiest of New Englanders, and Kelley gave up. The land lie fallow for over a century, owned but not really used by the Port of Portland, until the Parks Dept, bought the "Point" in 1984. This small patch of wooded sand dunes provides good boat watching opportunities, as you'll see many ocean-bound freighters pass by here. (And to think what might have been if Kelley succeeded!) Use

N Marine Drive to get there (there is a bike path paralleling the street). (sg)

Peninsula Park *located between N Ainsworth, N Kerby, N Portland Blvd, and N Albina* This North Portland oasis is known for its swimming pools, community center, gazebo-like octagonal bandstand, fountains. Its sunken rose gardens, with 65 varieties of roses, were actually the first in the city – even before the more famous International Rose Test Gardens. Sometimes spontaneous midnight picnics and sing-alongs can occur here. Three interesting historical asides about this park: 1) Originally owned by local businesswoman "Liverpool Liz", it had been the site for

Greetings from
PENINSULA PARK
NORTH PORTLAND

(sg)

a roadhouse and horse racetrack; 2) In the 1950s, the city zoo housed its penguins in the center's pool for six months because the zoo lacked the proper facilities when the birds arrived from Antarctica. Many Portlanders still remember calling it Penguin Park! and 3) Johnny Cash once had a picnic here (it's true!) (sg)

Skidmore Bluffs, also known as Mocks Crest Property *2206 N. Skidmore Terrace (west of Overlook Blvd)* We didn't include this li'l gem of a park in previous editions because we were jealous and preferred it to be our li'l secret. Well, what is popularly known as the "Skidmore Bluffs" is not so secret anymore. This is basically a patch of grass at the west end of Skidmore, sitting on Mocks Crest, the bluff overlooking the Willamette River below. You won't find softball fields or rose gardens here, just some of the best views in Portland. You'll have downtown and Forest Park on the opposite bank, and the industrial riverside areas and UP's Albina train yard directly below (which explains why this spot is popular with the hobos). It's a great spot to watch the sun set over the West Hills and contemplate life. (sg)

Performance and Art Spaces

Liberty Hall *311 N Ivy St. (just south of N Fremont) / 503-249-8888 /* Liberty Hall is a unique community space run collectively. Owned and operated by the Industrial Workers of the World, the Hall rents out office space to various groups and offers various events (live music, classes, film screenings, puppet shows, etc).

Mississippi Studios *3939 N. Mississippi Ave, Portland / 503-288-3895* This is a great place for live music (all shows 21+) in Portland, maybe the best. It features a small listening room and seats about 100 (so get tickets early). There's a bar in the back and a big patio where they show silent movies in the summer. Stellar sound courtesy of owner Jim Brunberg, who also runs the recording studio upstairs. They bring in a good range of acts from solo singer-songwriters to rock bands, jazz, bluegrass etc. They've even had Ricki Lee Jones and David Grisman here, as well as people like John Wesley Harding, Chris Smither, Steve Forbert, Tracy Grammer, Shivaree, Dirty Martini, and Guy Davis. Check it out! (jb)

Pizza

Pizza-A-Go-Go *3420 N Williams Ave. / 503-284-4674 / 11a-9p Su-Th, 11a-10p Fr-S* Don't let the cutesy name deceive you, they make a good pizza! Co-owned by the owner of Bella Faccia, this new joint makes a plethora of pies, all in the New Haven vein. For to-go slices, there's always cheese, pepperoni, a meat combo, veggie combo, and to the delight of many a zinester, a vegan combo (served seven days a week, no less!) They also offer delivery service and salads.

Restaurants

Beaterville Café *2201 N Killingsworth St. / 503-735-4652 / Mo-Fr 6a-3p, Sa-Su 8a-2* The Overlook neighborhood's favorite breakfast and lunch spot! You'll feel comfortable here, despite the fact that the place gets hella crowded on the weekends. There's always something cool to look at on the walls, whether it has to do with cars, bicycles, trains, planes, and other mechanical curiosities. And you can substitute tofu for eggs!

Flavour Spot *2310 N Lombard St. / 8 AM - 3 PM* Portland's best kept secret for deluxe breakfast waffling in the Video Chest parking lot! Great vegan options including vegan s'mores, vegan sausage, and peanut butter (3 kinds) and jelly! Or you can just chow down on a standard ham & cheese, or veggie sausage with smoked gouda, or any of

Mississippi Records (nb)

their other delicious delicacies! And remember people, just because it's sold off a cart just doesn't mean it's crappy but it does mean it's cheap ($2-4 ea)! (job)

Monsoon Thai   *4236 North Mississippi Avenue* Deceptively delicious Thai establishment tucked in the old Soup and Soap building on the corner of Skidmore and Mississippi. Deceptive in that they have an awful clipart Italian chef on the cover of their menu, play softrock hits that make your stomach turn, and decorate the place like your mom's pantry. But everything else, most importantly the food, is genuinely Thai. Moderately priced like most pdx Thai places, ~$7.50 a dish, and consistently delicious. (nb)

Record Stores

Mississippi Records   *4007 N Mississippi Ave / W-M 12-7 / 503-282-2990* Dense and well-stocked lil' gem of a record store on the burgeoning love it or hate it Mississippi Ave. Well priced and often hard-to-find vinyl, as well as cassettes and CDs, with listening station and friendly staff.

Small Grocery Stores

Big City Produce   *722 N Sumner St (at Albina) / 503-460-3830* Neighborhood produce store and more. Carries a wide range of organic and local produce as well as a smidgen of bulk items, medicinals and general foods. Excellent prices on produce and friendly atmosphere. (nb)

Video Stores

Videorama   *2310 N Lombard / (503)289-8408 / Mon-Fri 8am-11:30pm, Sat-Sun 9am-11:30pm*

Videorama (St. Johns)   *7522 N Lombard / (503)247-3433 / Mon-Fri 5am-11pm, Sat-Sun 6am-11pm*

Video Vérité   *3956 N. Mississippi Ave. / 503-445-9902 / Noon-11pm Daily* DVD-only rental store on Mississippi Ave with broad selection of arthouse, international, and classic films. Also host screenings in the basement.

Monsoon Thai (nb)

Northeast

Art Supplies

Collage *1639 NE Alberta St / (503) 249-2190* Locally owned, extensive arts and crafts store conveniently located on Alberta St. Friendly staff and competitive prices. Avoid riding your sporty roadbike all the way to the post-gentrified areas for sharpies. (nb)

Bars

Beaulahland *118 NE 28th Ave. / 503-235-2794* Friendly neighborhood bar and eatery that seems to be open non-stop. Great beer choices, good jukebox, pinball machines, and a pool table. Very popular trivia night on Tuesdays (starts at 9.30pm but get there early if you want a seat!) And now twice as large!

The KNOW *2022-26 NE Alberta St. / Daily 2p-6p, later for events* Once a super-cool multi-purpose arts space born out of the ashes that once was Gracie's, now the most happening bar on Alberta. How have the times changed. You will find here: art on display (new on Last Thursday), refreshments ($2 Iron City bottles), and a "microtheatre" that offers regular showings of independent art films for a nominal fee. Quite the spectacle.

Laurelwood Public House and Brewery *1728 NE 40th Av (at Sandy Blvd) / 503-282-0622 / Mo-Fr 11a-midnight Sa-Su 10a-midnight* If you want a more airy beer-drinking environment, the Laurelwood's high ceilings and spacious main room is the place to be. The food is pretty typical of brewpubs (i.e. not that cheap and not that spectacular) but the main point of a brewpub is the beer. And Laurelwood has some of the best in Portland. Check out their "Tree Hugger Porter" and "Free Range Red." If you go early for dinner, this place is kid-friendly, and there are a lot of local families that bring the little 'uns, so keep that in mind if you have a particular aversion to rugrats. (sg)

(aj)

Sandy Hut   *1430 NE Sandy Blvd / 503.235.7972* The Sandy Hut, affectionately referred to by desperate singles as the Handy Slut, is a close in NE bar and "restaurant" in a purple triangular (windowless) building on the South side of Sandy Boulevard, just off Burnside. Denizens tend to be rough and tumble, but it's hard to tell if that's actually how they are or if it's just an act put on by some hipsters that think it would be cool to go slumming. Greasy-ass food and an ok brew selection. This bar was put one step closer towards cult status when someone entered a car in the Portland Adult Soap Box Derby that was a striking replica. (sl)

Books, Zines, Comix and the like

In Other Words   *8 NE Killingsworth St / 503-232-6003 / Mo-Sa 10a-9p, Su 11a-6p* Your feminist, non-profit bookstore! In Other Words carries a diverse collection of women's writing, including tons of local grrl zines. Zine readings occur here from time to time. Once a fixture of Hawthorne, it is now located in Northeast with a larger space (and cheaper rent) which will mean a much-expanded selection!

Powell's Books at Portland International Airport.   *7000 NE Airport Way / 503-249-1950 / Oregon Market Location: Su-Fr 6a-10p, Sa 6a-7p; Concourse D Location: Daily 5a-3* You can make Powell's your first (or last) stop in Portland with this store! And there are two locations in the airport! If you don't have enough zines leaving town, stop in here to pick up a used Anne Rice paperback (you goth, you).

(cl)

Chain Grocery Stores, Supermarkets, etc.

Fred Meyer (Hollywood) *3030 NE Weidler St (south of Broadway) / 503-280-1300 / 7a-11p daily* This super-duper-market chain started out here way back in the day, but eventually got bought out by Ohio-based Kroger. Oh well. You can buy all your ordinary (and not so ordinary, they have an extensive line of natural foods as well) groceries here, as well as TVs, garden supplies, underwear, and bicycles. It's your all-purpose stop, and Jello Biafra once mentioned it too. The locals refer to it as "Freddies."

Fred Meyer (Glisan) *6615 NE Glisan St / 503-797-6940 / 7a-11p daily*

New Seasons (Concordia) *5320 NE 33rd Ave / 503-288-3838*

Trader Joe's (Hollywood District) *4218 NE Sandy Blvd / 503-284-1694 / 9a-9p daily*

Coffeehouses, Teahouses and the like

Black Cat Café *1203 NE Alberta St / 503.287.5908* Coffee and beer with lots of overstuffed couches and chairs. Free wi-fi, and for those who don't do the laptop thang, there are internet terminals as well (10 minutes free with drink purchase.) And don't forget the old-skool tabletop video games!

The Blend *2327 E Burnside St. / 503-234-8610 / Mo-Fr 7a-6p Sa-Su 8a-6p* (formerly "Beehive", formerly "Burnside Bean") Wow. This café has not gone through one, but two name changes since the last edition, due to it changing owners twice in the interim. The coffee here is good (Stumptown) but what makes Blend special is its atmosphere. The side room is a great, quiet place to spend your Sunday morning, whiling away the hours reading, writing, or drawing. They also have regular art showings. (sg)

Fuel Café *1452 NE Alberta St / 503-335-3835* Busy little café with good food at decent prices, cheap tea, and free internet (10 mins with drink purchase, also free wifi). Outdoor seating, yummy desserts, and great salads. Vegan/veggie friendly with meaty options also. (nb)

Goldrush Coffee Bar *2601 NE Martin Luther King Jr Blvd / 503-460-6657* This coffee joint makes some smooth coffee, and some nice sandwiches as well. Internet access available, and plenty of cool pictures of the neighborhood "back in the day" line the walls.

The Star-E-Rose *2403 NE Alberta St. / 503-249-812* The ol' standby coffee house of the burgeoning Alberta Arts District. A diverse menu, good coffee at decent prices (first refill of house is on the house, kids) and a relaxed feel is what you'll find here. Live music can be heard from time to time.

Tiny's Coffee (MLK) *2031 NE M L King Blvd / 503) 467-4199*

Donuts

Tonalis Doughnuts & Cream *2805 NE Alberta St / 503-284-4510 / open until midnight daily* In Portland's donut-verse, Voodoo reigns as king supreme and Annie's comes in second (for those initiated to Annie's ways). It's a shame that Tonalis gets forgotten about, because their donuts are really great. (I recommend the Buttermilk bars). And if it's summertime, they'll provide you with the ice cream to get through the hot days. Sure, it's not as hip as Voodoo, but the interior has an ambience of its own (reminding me of the east coast), and it's near all the things the kids on Alberta love to do. (sg)

Museums

Stark's Vacuum Museum *107 NE Grand Av / 800-230-4101 / M – F 8 am – 7 pm* A collection of old vacuums from the 1880s to 1960s, Many of which suck – as in don't or never worked so good. A fun excuse to learn the history of this common household machine. (cb)

Joan of Arc in Coe Circle, NE 39th & Glisan (al)

The Doghouse (aro)

Parks

Alberta Park *NE 22 & Killingsworth* Despite it's name, it is NOT located on Alberta St! Don't be fooled! Shady spaces, sports facilities, and Bike Polo (see listing under "bicycles") to be found here. Bounded by NE Killingsworth, NE Ainsworth, NE 19th, and NE 23rd.

Grant Park Grant Park, the neighborhood, is named after Grant Park, the park, named after Grant School, named after Grant, the president. Pretty exciting, huh? Grant Park (the park) is fairly ordinary as far as Portland parks go, except for one exceptional landmark--the Ramona the Brave Statue Garden. The protagonist for the popular series of children's books authored by Beverly Cleary, Ramona (and Cleary) adventured in this very neighborhood. Ramona's fictional residence was on NE Klickitat St, just a few blocks north of the park. In fact, some of Ramona's adventures involve this park! In 1995, Portland immortalized Ramona, her friend Henry, and her dog Ribsy by placing these bronze statues here. (sg)

Irving Park *between NE Fremont, NE 11th, NE Siskyou, and NE 7th* Possibly Northeast's most popular park. Ball fields, picnic benches, gorgeous trees, basketball courts, and crazed dogs populate this green spot (off-leash area).

Pizza

Bella Faccia Pizzeria *2934 NE Alberta St. / 503-282-0600 / 11:30a-10p daily*
Forget New York, let's talk New Haven style! For the uninitiated, the Big Apple is not the
only city to take pride in its pizza. And sure, New Haven, CT style pizza is quite similar
to NYC, but I think New Havenites take more pride in their product. The generations-
running feud between Elm City fixtures Pepe's and Sally's over who makes a better pie
is legendary, and known nation-wide. Bella Faccia carries the spirit of New Haven pizza
to the Alberta Arts District. Firstly, the yardstick for pizza measurement is the cheese
slice. You can dress it up as much as you want, but if a pizzeria can't make a good
cheese slice, then it can't make pizza. Bella doesn't disappoint there! Secondly, it also
makes tasty gourmet pies as well. Thirdly, Bella offers damn good vegan slices seven
days a week, loaded with choice veggies and seasoned tempeh on a bean base (now all
y'all who were rolling yer eyes at the intro are all at attention, huh!) Finally, the owner is
actually from the New Haven area (so she obviously knows what good pizza is!)And the
ambience of the place: pure magic! They always have some interesting music playing.
The other day they were playing Electric Light Orchestra. ELO, man!!

Record Stores

Everyday Music (Sandy) *1931 NE Sandy Blvd / 503-239-7610*

Restaurants

The Doghouse *2845 E. Burnside (in Wild Oats parking lot) / 503 239-3647, fax 503
239 / 11a-9p daily* Who doesn't love The Doghouse? The best hot dog fixin's in town,
totally friendly service and more than a couple veggie options! My fave is the veggie
Italian sausage dog with sauerkraut and jalepeños. They serve them "Chicago style" and
offer veggie chilidogs. Small place that offers drive thru and ordering at the window with
some picnic tables out front. The Doghouse rules!! (kd)

Don Pancho Taqueria *2002 NE Alberta / 503-459-4247* Homemade and super-
cheap with vegan, vegetarian and meat-tastic offerings. Very friendly folks. A welcome
alternative to the ol' standbys up the street (La Bonita and La Serenita). (nb)

El Taco Express #2 *5447 NE 42nd Ave / 503-284-8446* Home of the best (albeit
drippy) chile relleno burrito and the new crown for the biggest, cheapest, tastiest veggie
burrito post La Fonda. Extensive menu and dirtcheap prices -- an all-around authentic
taqueria (eg: the womens bathroom light switch controls the dining room lights, too).
(nb)

Halo Thai *1625 NE Alberta / 503-546-7063 / M-Th 11-9:30, Fr-Sat 11-10pm, Closed
Sun* Family-run Thai restaurant, featuring handcrafted curries and a tasty Pad Thai.
I find myself wishing the meals were simpler and more vibrantly fresh, as I think Thai
should be, but the presentation is well-done (both food & atmosphere) and sometimes
the food matches up. (nb)

Koji's Osakaya (Broadway)   *1502 NE Weidler / (503) 280-0992*

La Serenita   *2817 NE Alberta St. / 503-335-8283*   One of Portland's most popular Mexican taqueria. The only catch is that it may or may not be veggie friendly (is there lard in the beans?). If you are of the vegetarian/vegan persuasion, you should play safe and go next door to La Bonita (2839 NE Alberta, 503.281.3662) which also serves up the Mexican "authentico", sans the lardo.

Paulsen's United Drugs   *4246 NE Sandy Blvd / 503-287-1163 / Mo-Fr 9a-6:30p, Sa 9a-5p*   This pharmacy has been around since 1918, clearly making it "old school". And what better way to show off its old schoolness than by still having a working soda fountain? Come in to get an ice cream soda or cherry phosphate, and enjoy the free Wi-Fi service. (sg)

Vita Café   *3024 NE Alberta St. / 503-335-823*   The Paradox's sister eatery in the northeast. Vita's menu is basically the same as the Paradox, with some additions (like Vegan Chicken Fried Steak with gravy! Mmmmm) to make it worth your while to check out.

Small Grocery Stores

Alberta Co-op Grocery   *1500 NE Alberta St / 503-287-4833*   This small grocery began as a neighborhood natural food ordering club. Good selection of local organic produce and baked goods, as well as the typical health food store selection of bulk items, medicinals and general foods. Decent prices, especially on vegetables. Support local co-ops!

Theaters

Hollywood Theatre   *4122 NE Sandy Blvd / 503-281-4215*   Built by architects Bennes & Herzog in the grand Baroque and Gothic Eclectic styles for Fox, the 1500 seat Hollywood opened its doors on July 17, 1926 with the film More Pay-Less Work. The

Hollywood Theatre (lg)

(sg)

Hollywood was-and is-one of the most ornate movie palaces in the Pacific Northwest, built in a time when theaters were meant to stand out. With its unique Byzantine rococo tower, the theater quickly became a fixture in the neighborhood, so much so that the commercial district along Sandy surrounding the Hollywood was named after it (not the other way around!), the only time a neighborhood in Portland was named after a building. Like the Bagdad, the Hollywood started as a cinema/vaudeville house, but switched to all movies sometime mid-century. The Hollywood got into the widescreen game, when in the early 1960's it became Cinerama-capable. In 1975, to better compete with the cineplex competition, the balcony was converted into two smaller theaters, a setup that remains to this day. This wasn't enough, though, and the Hollywood went through its slump years. The turnaround came in April of 1997, when the Oregon Film & Video Foundation bought the ailing cinema. Committed to restoring the Hollywood to its original luster, its new owners have been extensively renovating the theater inside and out. Hopefully in the near future they will be able to remove the red floor-to-ceiling draperies in the main theater and restore the deco interior that hides behind it. Currently the Hollywood shows an eclectic mix of international. indie-arthouse, and local films, and hosts various film festivals. Four dollar movie night on Monday! (sg)

Kennedy School *5736 NE 33rd Ave. / 503-249-3983* Opened in 1915 and closed due to disrepair in 1980, McMenamins renovated the school into an arty neighborhood hub with restaurant, 3 specialty bars, lodging ($$!), hot tubs, brewhouse and gym. Most locals know it for the budget theater/pub ($3 movies) with old couches and easy chairs. The building is fun to explore with lots of creepy art. Tasty beer & pizza, but the rest of the food is notoriously sub-par. (nb)

Laurelhurst Theater *2735 E Burnside St / 503-238-4088* Built in 1923, the Laurelhurst was one of the first art-deco styled buildings to grace the City of Roses. It served as a neighborhood cinema throughout the years, but the Cineplex era brought upon the Laurelhurst hard times. The Laurelhurst tried everything they could to stay afloat. In 1979, the theater was divided into four smaller screening rooms (the current format we have today) to compete with the cineplexes, but it didn't do much. During the 80's and 90's, the Laurelhurst stuck with a cheap-ticket, B-movie and second-run format and earned the nickname "The Urine-Hurst" due to the state of its clientele (and surrounding neighborhood). Around 2000 the theater was bought and renovated by the current owners. The single-screen became a four-screen format, and like the Bagdad, the Laurelhurst serves beer and pizza. With a renewed sense of respect, the Laurelhurst has become a community hub again for the surrounding Kerns/Buckman neighborhood and the jumpin' commercial district along 28th Ave. (sg)

Thrift Stores

Value Village Hollywood *4420 NE Hancock St / M-Sat 9-9, Sun 10-7* Yes, this is part of a major national chain, but the store is huge, well lit, and clothing is sorted by size and color. Every day there is a color tag discount and the prices are reasonable. Even the parking lot is huge. Very hard to dislike! (en)

Video Stores

Videorama (Alberta) *2640 NE Alberta St / 503) 288-4067 / Mon-Fri 6am-11pm, Sat-Sun 8am-11pm* One of the first video stores in Portland, Videorama has

Alberta Cooperative Grocery

(nb)

supplied the video-hungry holed up on (ubiquitous) rainy days since 1984. I can only speak for the Alberta location, but it's incredibly well-stocked and has very knowledgeable and friendly staff. Quite refreshing after dealing with the highschool flunkies you find at Blockbuster and Hollywood. Besides, you support a local Portland business who gives to local charities and reinvests in the community. New releases are $3.50 and oldies are $2.50 for 5 days. (nb)

Art Supplies

I've Been Framed *4950 SE Foster Rd / (503) 775-2651* This gem of an art shop is found at the unlikely intersection of Foster and Powell. Possibly some of the cheapest finds in the area, with a really friendly staff. Unlike places like Utrecht, I've Been Framed focuses less on a standardized selection and more on closeouts they get for cheap. So you'll never know what you'll find here! (sg)

Muse Art and Design *4224 SE Hawthorne Blvd / 503.231.8704 / 10am-6pm mo-sa, 12pm-5pm su* Finally! An art supply shop on Hawthorne! Muse is a nice li'l art supply store that will keep most artists satisfied. They also have a free library containing titles on art, artists, techniques, materials, and eclectic visual references, plus exhibit art by local artists. (sg)

Bars

Angelo's *4620 SE Hawthorne Blvd. / 503-231-0337* Comfortably situated on the outskirts of the sometimes irritating Hawthorne District, Angelo's offers $2 pint specials, free pool, buttrock jukebox (you know what we mean), pinball and friendly bartenders. Nate used to ride almost

(un)

Southeast

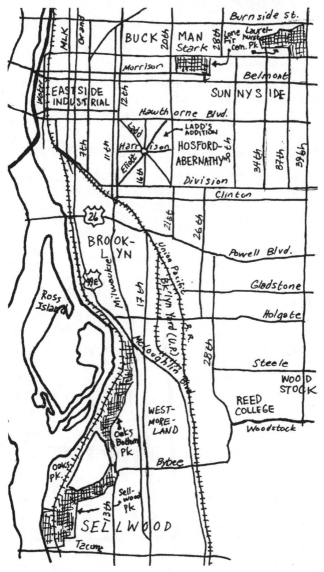

90 blocks on a regular basis to frequent this bar, sometimes even through blistering summer heat or torrential downpours (and he doesn't even have fenders on his bike!). But he got alcohol poisoning (not from Angelos, from his high school reunion...long story) and now has the straightedge, maybe.

Basement Pub *1028 SE 12th Ave / 503-231-6068* A little of everything good you would want in a bar. Great food deals, some dishes as low as a dollar! Dollar-fifty Pabst, and Laurelwood Beer! Also hosts trivia night on Sundays at 9.30 pm which is quite popular. Get there early if you want to participate.

The Vern (a.k.a. Hanigan's) *2622 SE Belmont St. / 503-233-7851* Look for the TAVERN sign with the "T" and the "A" burnt out. Though not quite the dive it used to be, still comfortably in the dive category: cheap beer, free/$.25 pool, good jukebox, holes in the bathroom wall.. what else do you want?

Books, Zines, Comix and the like

Excalibur Comics *2444 SE Hawthorne Blvd. / 503-231-7351 / Mo-Th 11a-8p, Fr-Sa 10a-8p, Su 11a-7p* If the "alternative" comix selection at Reading Frenzy just isn't cutting it for ya, because maybe, just maybe, you want the newest issue of Green Lantern, then head here. Excalibur is probably the best (and oldest, since 1976) of the traditional comic book stores in town (the other comic shops in Portland are pretty scary places).

I mean, c'mon! They got Howard the Duck pulling a sword out of a stone on their sign (illustration done by Frank Brunner, the original Howard the Duck artist!) How old school can you get? Pick up your Marvel Comics fix, get some backing boards, argue with the counter-jock about the Fantastic Four movie, and get in a debate about who would win in a fight: Wolverine or Spawn? (If you are a comics geek, you will understand every damn word I just said). They have a decent selection of alt-comix as well. And don't forget, new comics day is Wednesday! (sg)

Guapo Comics *6416 SE Foster Road / 503-772-3638 / daily 11am-8pm* After too many years of Portland being a "comics" town with a lack of comics stores, it's nice to see things change for the better. This recently opened shop on Foster may seem a bit "out there"

(na)

(na)

(especially since everyone hip lives north of Fremont these days, doncha know), but it is well worth the trip, especially if you combine it with a visit to I've Been Framed. The two owners are sweet and friendly, and the shop carries a good selection of mainstream, alternative, and mini-comics. Keep an eye out, they hope to open a café in the space soon!

Powell's on Hawthorne *3723 SE Hawthorne Blvd. / 503-238-1668 / Mo-Th 9a-10p, Fr-Sa 9a-11p, Su 9a-9* An all-purpose version (albeit smaller) of the main store, divided into three rooms. Also includes the ever-popular Fresh Pot (see separate listing).

Powell's Books for Cooks and Gardeners *3747 SE Hawthorne Blvd. / 503-235-3802 / Mo-Sa 9a-9p Su 9a-8* Just what the name says! The largest store of its kind in the country. Also connected to Pastaworks.

Chain Grocery Stores, Supermarkets, etc.

Fred Meyer (Hawthorne) *3805 SE Hawthorne Blvd / 503-872-3300 / 7a-11p daily*

New Seasons (Seven Corners) *1954 SE Division St / 503-445-2888 / Daily 7a-11p* These upscale groceries were started in 1999 by the former owners of Nature's Northwest. These stores are a weird hybrid offering the healthy, fancy foods of Whole Foods and the co-ops, while also offering the more standard grocery store fare of Safeway and Freddy's as well. New Seasons is being aggressive about opening new stores, and caught a bit of controversy with opening of Seven Corners, a mere six blocks from Peoples Co-Op. Two things to point out: New Seasons has the best samples on the weekends, offering up tons of fruit, cheese, bread, cooked food, and sometimes beer! And New Seasons is the only place in Portland to find Moxie and Vernors.

New Seasons (Sellwood) *1214 SE Tacoma St / 503-230-4949*

Trader Joe's (Southeast) *4715 SE. 39th Ave / 503-777-1601 / 9a-9p daily*
National chain of unique and inexpensive gourmet groceries. Not the best place for all-around shopping (their produce section is sparse, and they lack the bulk-foods section that Wild Oats, New Seasons and the co-ops feature), but great for finding deals on stuff (including the ubiquitous Three Buck Chuck). Good beer selection too. If you are so inclined, their frozen microwaveable foods are some of the best ever.

Coffeehouses, Teahouses and the like

The Fresh Pot (Hawthorne-Powells) *3729 SE Hawthorne Blvd (inside Powell's on Hawthorne) / 503-232-8928* Fresh Pot is an amazing little coffeeshop. You are bound to run into someone you know here (even if you're not from Portland!) and possibly the person behind the counter once lived with you. They've got lovely hardwood floors and large windows that you can sit in. Their coffee is the best in town, rivaled only by Stumptown itself (their supplier). You are guaranteed a velvet-like froth on top of any soy latté, and there are plenty of charming baristas to gape at as you eat your pastries and slurp your coffee. Very zinester friendly. Wireless internet, so bring your laptop. (ng)

Gladstone Coffee House *3813 SE Gladstone St / (503) 775-1537* Located on the not-hip-at-all stretch of Gladstone (wait...is there a hip stretch of Gladstone?), this coffee joint is a respite for the neighborhood and a getaway for those of us who get sick of bumping into everyone we know at the more trafficked places "up north". Owned by the same folks who brought us the Albina Green, you'll find Stumptown Coffee and

(cl)

(cl)

pastries, plus time to actually complete the project you're working on rather than having to confront your ex. (Lover, roommate, worker, take your pick.) (sg)

Haven Coffee *3551 SE Division S / (503) 236-6890 / 7:30 am-7:30 pm every day*
Quiet and roomy joint that serves up Stumptown Coffee and snacks. A great place to sit and draw while waiting for the rain to stop...it ends, right? (sg)

Mojo's Coffee Den *2853 SE Stark St. / 503-238-8891* Small neighborhood coffee shop that serves coffee, tea, pastries and smoothies. Feels often like hanging out in your own living room or on a best friend's porch, especially since everyone seems to know each other. Smoking outside only.

Muddy Waters Coffeehouse *2908 SE Belmont St / 503-233-1923 / Mo-Sa 7a-10p Su 8a-9p* You may think last thing this part of town needs is another coffee joint. But I always say there's room for more good coffee places, especially to counter the corporate (or wanna-be corporate) coffee infiltrating inner SE. (And yes, this includes Peet's.) Muddy Waters is a welcome addition to Belmont. Great coffee, cozy atmosphere, friendly staff, and a decent food selection. This is the type of place that encourages you to while away the day. No relation to the overrated java joint in San Francisco. (sg)

Palio *1996 SE Ladd Ave. (at Ladd Circle) / 503-232-9412 / Mo-Sa 7a-11p, Su 9a-11* This place rocks for location ... smack dab in the middle of the Ladd's Addition! It's a little treat oasis that serves tasty desserts (mostly cakes) from Ja Civa Chocolateer, coffee & tea, and sometimes-delectable milkshakes in the summer. Outdoor seating and late night hours make this a great destination for that walk or bike ride you wanted to take. Added bonus: the best alleys in SE Portland surround you. (rg)

The Pied Cow *3244 SE Belmont St / 503-230-4866 / Tu-Th 4p-12a, Fr 4p-1a, Sa 10a-1a* If you're not satisfied with a typical coffee house and want more of an "experience" then come here. Located in a beautifully restored Victorian house, the Pied Cow serves some of the best hot drinks around. Espresso-based beverages are delicious and inexpensive (but HOT! Be careful of their glasses). Wine and beer are also available. The décor inside is quite funky, and in the summertime you can sit outside in the garden, and even share a fancy-tastic (tobacco-fueled, of course) hookah. Good place to bring your out-of-town guests or someone you want to impress.

Red and Black Coffee Collective *2131 SE Division St. / 503-231-389* This collectively worker-owned café has plenty of table space, couches, and computers in the back. Good vegetarian sandwiches, food, beer, and they roast their coffee at the café. Live music and all ages shows practically every night of the week, and IWW socials on Sunday afternoons. A good place to hang out and discuss ideas for your next zine.

Redwing Coffee and Baking *1700 SE 6th Ave / 503-445-9900 / Mon-Fri 6:30 am-8pm, closed weekends* Tucked away in inner SE, this cooperatively owned coffeeshop is not only beautiful to look at, they have great (& cheap!) homemade soups, sandwiches, baked goods and coffee roasted right there in the shop. Veggie & vegan friendly, free wifi, and some of the best bathrooms in town. Also conveneniently located a vblock from the Goodwill Superstore. (nb)

Rimsky-Korsakoffee House *707 SE 12th Ave / 503-232-2640 / 7pm-midnight Sun-Thu, 7pm-1am Fri-Sat* A quirky and fun coffee and dessert place in an old house in SE. There are odd things afoot here, but I won't tell you, I don't want to spoil it... just keep your eyes open. Amazing desserts, coffee and tea; this is a great place to spend some time. Sometimes there is live classical music, and one Sunday a month the church of craft congregates here. Note that it's only open in the evenings!. (kd)

(tr)

(nb)

Stumptown Coffee Roasters (Division) *4525 SE Division St / 503-230-7702 / Mo-Fr 6a-6p, Sa-Su 7a-7p* The guaranteed best cup of French pressed coffee you'll find in Portland. And the espresso is smoother than a secret smooch (!!). The owner buys directly from small coffee farms (many organic, all fair trade), and they roast their beans fresh every day. Yum. Three locations satisfy your every mood – spread out and play Scrabble at the original Division store, gossip on the couches with your friends; wear your best outfit to get an urban cup o' joe at the Belmont café; or observe the business-people running endlessly from here to there at the Downtown location (which also serves wine and beer). Check out the cool art shows at all three. (rg)

Stumptown Coffee Roasters (Belmont) *3356 SE Belmont St / 503-232-8889 / Mo-Fr 6a-9p, Sa-Su 7a-9p*

Tao of Tea *3430 SE Belmont St. / 503-736-0198 / Daily 11a-11* Huge selection of tea, Asian style snacks, and a calm atmosphere. They are also a tea wholesaler, so order online.

Three Friends Coffeehouse and Café *201 SE 12th Ave. / 503-236-6411* Three Friends is an independent coffee joint with friendly servers and a relaxed atmosphere. Often hosting events organized by Portland's progressive and Queer sets, Three Friends also offers a comfortable place to write, draw, read or meet a friend. Perks: close-in and within 2 blocks of four bus lines, internet access, Stumptown coffee, vegan conscious, pool table, and reasonable prices.

Tiny's Coffee *1412 SE 12th / 503-239-5859 / Mon-Th 6a-10p, Fr 6a-12a, Sa 7a-12a, Su 7a-10p* Stumptown coffee, good food (including some strange menu items), videogames, pinball, lively staff, wifi. Inviting neighborhood feel, often with good music playing, monthly art openings, and a nice back patio. (nb)

Ever-nebulous "Other" Category

Twilight Rummage Sale at The Eagles Lodge *4904 SE Hawthorne Blvd.* Once a month people gather at The Eagles Lodge to sell their collectibles, wares, and crafts. The people who organize this make sure to always have a good turn around of merchants, so you don't always see the same thing. The crowd is an amazing collection of young and old, collectors and browsers and Eagles Lodge members. But the thing that can't be overstated: you can rummage and shop while drinking a beer and listening to dj's spinning great vintage tunes! Also, if you need some food or a smoke, it's just a few steps to the bar. Veggie corn dogs and burgers available. Since it is 5-9pm, The Twilight Rummage Sale is a great way to start off a Saturday night. (kd)

Hostels

Hostelling International-Portland, Hawthorne District *3031 SE Hawthorne Blvd. / 503-236-3380 / Office hours: 8am-10pm daily* Although a bit further from downtown than the Northwest Neighborhood hostel, it's still easy to get to (use the 14 bus) and close to all the wonders Hawthorne Blvd brings. Friendly staff, clean decor, spacious kitchen & living rooms, yard, garden, deck, covered porch, and an ecoroof! Linens included, no lockout/curfew, bike storage, bike rental, ample free parking, Internet (DSL kiosk & wireless system), free baked goodies, $1 pancake breakfasts, and a Sunday Brunch open to the community. Dorm rate: $17-22, private room rate: $40-48 (higher price in summer), plus lodging tax and a $3 fee if you are not a Hosteling International member. Open all year with 24-hour access. Reservations are advisable during the summer and on weekends. Reservations accepted by phone, mail, fax, and e-mail. Toll free number is (866) 447-3031. (sg)

Late Night Eats

Fireside Coffee Lodge *1223 SE Powell Blvd. / 503-230-8987 / 24-7 operation* Largely unknown (probably due to it being on uber-pedestrian-unfriendly US 26), this all-night coffee shop features "rustic" décor, (though some of the "animal" decor may offend some people) wired and wireless internet service, and of course, coffee. A unique feature here is the "study room" where one can go to drink and work in privacy.

Original Hotcake & Steak House *1002 SE Powell Blvd* The food is horrible and don't look anyone directly in the eye or you might have a fight on hand. We heartily don't recommend going here, unless you are totally desparate. But it's open 24 hours and we have to fill up this space somehow.

Museums

Kidd's Toy Museum   *1327 SE Grand Av / 503-233-7807 / M – F 10 am – 5:30 pm, Sat 10 am – 1 pm* A "Secret" Museum tucked inside of an Auto Supply Store. There is just a little sign on the outside, otherwise you could walk by and never know that just inside is a plethora of toy mechanical banks, dolls, toy cars, and much more from the 1860s to 1930s. F. E. Kidd has gathered one of the largest private toy collections in the nation. Across the street and in the adjacent storefront you'll find more of the collection. FREE ADMISSION! (cb)

The Historic Belmont Firehouse-Safety Learning Center and Fire Museum   *900 SE 35th Street (at Belmont) / 503-823-3615 / by appointment, some Saturday open houses* Slide down a fireman's pole. See a historic fire truck next to a modern one. Ring the Alarm Bell. Fun and interactive museum teaching us about fire-fighting and safety. Collection will move to a new Museum & Safety Learning Center being planned for downtown Waterfront (2008?) (cb)

Other Mercantile-type Operations

Andy and Bax   *324 SE Grand Av / (503) 234-7538 / 9a-6p Mo-Th, 9a-9p Fr, 9a-6pm Sa* Portland's oldest army-navy store, since 1947! It's got most everything you need for clothing oneself and for urban expeditioning. I end up here quite often. It's my favorite place for winter wear: all the hats, wooly socks, gloves, wool pants, and thermal underwear you can possibly need. Like most army-navy joints, there's a bounty of surplus clothing items for cheap. Who knows what values lie in them there bins? And if Bush comes back to town, this is where you can pick up gas masks so you don't get tear-gassed! (sg)

(aro)

Parks

Col. Summers Park *1925 SE Taylor St* The Buckman neighborhood's local park, named after a hero of some war. (And watch out! People commonly mis-spell it as SumNer.) There's hella sports facilities here, including tennis court, baseball field, and basketball court. There's also a community garden, and if you're lucky, you might catch crazed folks playing Bike Polo here. (see listing under "bicycles") Bounded by SE Belmont, SE Taylor, SE 17th and SE 20th.

Creston Park *SE 44 Av & SE Powell Blvd* Despite being on major traffic artery Powell Blvd, Creston Park's tall Douglas Firs and landscaping provide a shady respite from the urban world. Plenty of room for a picnic or a dog walk can be found here, plus a pool to splash around on a warm summer day. (sg)

Crystal Springs Rhododendron Garden *SE 28 Avenue, one block north of Woodstock Blvd. / 503-771-8386* Located on seven acres just west of Reed College, Crystal Springs Rhododendron Garden features more than 2,500 rhododendrons, azaleas, and companion plants. Spring-fed Crystal Springs Lake surrounds much of the garden, attracting many species of birds and waterfowl. The winding paths and wooded knolls provide good places to get away and have personal time, if you want. The one drawback is the admission charge. Admission is free to all from Labor Day through February. A $3 admission fee is charged between 10:00am-6:00pm, Thursday through Monday, March through Labor Day. And sometimes there's simply no one at the gate! (sg)

Laurelhurst Park (sg)

Eastbank Esplanade A path lying along the east bank of the Willamette River between the Steel and Hawthorne, just opened back in 2001. This area was full of warehouses too, just like on the westside, and they were also torn down in the 60's to make way for a freeway (Interstate 5). But unfortunately, that freeway still remains. But, they did manage to build a pathway regardless. Now you can cruise both banks of the river! There are some cool historical markers along the path. And the 1,200 ft. long floating walkway (just north of the Burnside Bridge) is the longest floating walkway in the United States. Waterfront Park is connected to the Eastbank Esplande by the pathways along the Steel Bridge (lower deck) and Hawthorne Bridge. (sg)

Kenilworth Park *SE 34 Ave and SE Holgate Blvd* Kenilworth Park was built in the teens, and it reflects the "City Beautiful" design sense of the time. Its curvy paths, tall trees, and the grassy ravine at the north end make it like a Laurelhurst in miniature. There is also a great overlook on the west side where you can catch the sun setting. (sg)

Laurelhurst Park *Bound by SE Ankeny, SE 39th, SE Stark, and SE 33rd* The land of happy people and happy dogs and happy trees and happy swans. I think you will feel good there. The park was designed by the Olmsted family (think Central Park and Chicago's ring of parks) over a hundred years ago. Woodsy and secluded feeling, yet minutes from "happening" Belmont and Hawthorne commercial districts. (kd)

Lone Fir Cemetery *Bounded by SE Stark, SE Morrison, SE 20th, and SE 26th* Old cemetery filled with pioneers, lumberjacks, beloved mothers, and soldiers. A bit of Portland history in this small cemetery that has some beautiful tombstones, statues, and lots of shady trees. Fun to hang out in day or night. Entrance at SE 26th. (kd)

Mount Tabor This 643 foot high hill was formed by volcanic activity. In fact, it is an extinct volcano, the only extinct volcano to be found within city limits in the U.S! This mount could have been eaten up by the expanding development of the city of Portland, but famed park designers the Olmstead Brothers recognized the significance of this place, and urged the city to protect Mount Tabor in the form of a park. We can thank them today for their foresight, because Tabor has one of the best viewpoints of the city. And its forested slopes are a great place to unwind. The windy road on the westside is closed to traffic, so it's a great place to "bomb" (to appropriate the Zoobomber's lingo). All auto traffic is barred from the park on Wednesday, even! The beautiful open reservoirs were slated to be covered though (in the name of "stopping terrorism"), irking many a neighborhood resident. But now that's all just a bad memory. Access from SE Salmon east of SE 60th, or from the east at SE Harrison west of SE 70th. (sg)

The Springwater Corridor Trail This linear park starts on the east edge of the Sellwood neighborhood in the SE and goes all the way to the exotic town of Boring (yes, that IS its real name.) This route was originally a trolley line (alternately known as the the "Springwater" line or the "Bellrose" line) built in 1903 and discontinued in 1958. In

Looking toward Mt. Tabor (dw)

the 1990's, the city of Portland and Metro (the regional body of government) acquired the unused rail line and converted it into a park. Now instead of steel rails and ties, we have a paved 10 foot wide path that you can walk, bike, skateboard, etc. etc.

The length of the path is approximately 16 miles long, and the main entrance (trailhead) is at SE 45th at SE Johnson Creek Blvd. There is a "sneak" entrance to the trail at the end of SE Berkeley (just keep on going past the racquet club nonsense) off of SE Tacoma. (For you thrift kids, this is on the other side of the Union Pacific tracks by the Goodwill Bins!) In the end of 2006, this trail will fully connect to the OMSI-Springwater Trail (see Oaks Bottom listing) via a series of bridges spanning 99E, the UP railroad tracks, and Johnson Creek. When that happens, we'll have a 21-mile long path, reaching from downtown Portland to Boring! Until then, you'll have to use a somewhat-tricky street connection via SE Spokane St to get between the two.

Performance and Art Spaces

Cinema Project *New American Art Union, 922 SE Ankeny (for screenings), PO Box 5991, Portland, OR 97228 (mail) / 503-232-8269 / screenings every other week, 7:30pm, Sept‹May* Cinema Project is a collectively run screening series highlighting innovative film work, both historical and contemporary, by well recognized and accomplished artists from around the world. They make an effort to bring artists to present their work in person, and in almost all cases, the work they show has never been screened in Portland or the Pacific Northwest for that matter. Cinema Project operates seasonally (programming in the Fall takes place between September and December and Spring season goes from late February through May). They also collaborate regularly with other arts groups in town that can happen in other locations.

Oddball Studios   *2138 E Burnside St. / 503-231-1344 / Mo-Sa 11a-7p, Su 12p-6*
Oddball is a tattoo studio, but if you aren't into getting your "piece" worked on while you're in town, you can stop in to see artwork on their walls. They have new artists up monthly, on the First Saturday artwalk (see artwalk).

Pizza

Hot Lips Pizza (Hawthorne)   *2211 SE Hawthorne Blvd / 503-234-9999 / Mo-Th 11a-10p, Fr-Sa 11a-11p, Su 11:30a-10p*

Stark Naked Pizza   *2835 SE Stark St / 503-459-4450` / Daily 11:30a-11:00p* One of my favorite attributes of the New Rose City is its ability to tackle problems effectively. One long standing problem in town is the shortage of East Coast style pizzerias, especially in SE. But thankfully over the past few years some really choice pizzerias have been opening up. Newest to the list, and the first one to come into SE (excepting Hot Lips on Hawthorne) is Stark Naked. Delicious thin-crust pies, with just the right amount of sauce and cheese. Their slices are only $2, the lowest priced amongst the East Coast styles. (sg)

Hawthorne Blvd, looking west from SW 38th (dw)

Record Stores

Discourage Records

1737 SE Morrison St. / 503-528-1098 / Tu-Su 11a-7 A record collector's paradise. This store would be the place to search for that punk record that has alluded you for years. (Maybe they have it in pink vinyl?) They also do business online. Make sure you check out their outdoor posting board, which sometimes features amusing communiqués with customers. (sg)

Jackpot Records (Hawthorne)

3736 SE Hawthorne Blvd / 503-239-7561 / Mo-Th 10a-7p, Fr-Sa 10a-8p, Su 11a-6p Probably Portland's most infamous indie record store, with a large vinyl selection.

Paradox Café (nb)

Music Millennium (Eastside)

3158 E Burnside St / 503-231-8926 / 10a-10p Mo-Sa, 11a-9p Su One of the largest independent record retailers in the U.S. They have three locations to serve you well. The westside store also offers a lot of in-store shows on a regular basis (at least one every two weeks), which have featured the likes of Paul Westerberg and Joe Strummer.

Music Millenium (Classical)

3144 E Burnside St / 503-231-8909 / 10a-10p Mo-Sa, 11a-9p Su

Q is for Choir

2510 SE Clinton St. at SE 26th / 503-235-967 Record and zine store that also stocks turntables, a healthy bookshelf, and zines. Has a great variety and selection. I always find things that I didn't know I was looking for. (job)

Restaurants

Cup n Saucer *3566 SE Hawthorne Blvd. / 503-236-6001* Vegan friendly diner fare. Breakfast served all day. Revolving art exhibits.

Dots *2521 SE Clinton St. at SE 26th / 503-235-0203* This neat bar/restaurant located in the heart of the Clinton neighborhood has dark ambience and comfy booth seating.

Juniors Café (ng)

The velvet wallpaper and velvet big-eyed children paintings are all the rage with the Pabst set. Veggie and vegan options are offered alongside traditional diner fare. They serve food late into the eve, but access is restricted to 21 and over past ten.

Foti's Greek Deli   *1740 E Burnside St. / 503-232-0274*   Buy pita and humus for two bucks, or, for a few dollars more, you can get a garden burger rumored to be the best ever!

Fujin Café   *3549 SE Hawthorne Blvd. / 503-231-3753 / Daily 11a-9p*   The crispy eggplant is something very different. I bring my own containers and they pack me up to go.

Hoda's Middle Eastern Cuisine   *3401 SE Belmont St. / 503-236-8325*   Middle-Eastern café specializing in tasty food at low costs. The place can be quite packed on the weekends, though.

Junior's   *1742 SE 12th Ave. / 503-235-547*   Breakfast and lunch served up by the same people at Dots. Great breakfast fare and vegan friendly. Located on the outer perimeter of Ladd's Addition. Closes at 3pm.

La Villa   *SE Morrison between SE 7th and 8th*   New-ish Middle-Eastern restaurant that features $3 falafel sandwiches! That's the cheapest I found in town so far! You can't beat that with a stick! And they're good! Plus, they have fried califlour and eggplant, and zattar bread, which I haven't seen since Montreal! The only thing is, they always want to get you to buy the Super Falafel sandwich for $4.95, so be warned.

Laughing Planet   *3320 SE Belmont St. / 503-235-6472 / Mo-Sa 11a-10p, Su 11a-9p*   They make a fine n' dandy bean & cheese burrito that's only $3.25, but Laughing Planet excels in the art of making "fancy burritos", using feta cheese, broccoli, jicama and even SPAM as ingredients (even cactus occasionally!) Tofu, soy cheese, and vegan sour cream are also available. So yeah, they're not "authentica", but there's other places in town you can go for that. While you're there, check out all the R. Crumb reproductions on the wall.

Nicholas' Restaurant *318 SE Grand Ave. / 503-235-512* Traditional and delicious Mediterranean fare. Vegan mezza option, and they even offer vegan baklava! (If you don't mind honey.) Tiny, very popular, and tends to fill up fast, so come early.

Paradox *3439 SE Belmont at SE 35th / 503-232-750* The vegan/vegetarian mecca of the southeast (Portland, that is). The Paradox specializes in inexpensive meatless meals, though they do offer a real hamburger (cooked on a separate grill), hence the paradox. They also serve their breakfast all day! There has been some grumblings in the zine community about the recent price increases, but they still do offer fat (or is it phat!) servings for your dollar. The weekend brunch hours are hella crowded, so plan accordingly. Right next to Wunderland.

Small Grocery Stores

Food Fight! Vegan Grocery Store *4179 SE Division / 233-3910* Food Fight is a wonderful and brilliant thing. Not just because the owners are super nice and so helpful or because everything in the store is animal product free or because there are so many yummy things you regularly buy and things you have never seen before there; no, the number one reason Food Fight is amazing and brilliant is the mystery asian fake meats! They are so good, things like mushroom cake and golden roast and ham, and others which are even more mysterious and are all written in another language. All of them are vegan and all are good. Food Fight is a great addition to Portland.

Limbo *707 SE 39th Ave. / 503-774-8008* A small organic and locally-grown produce market, conveniently located next to Trader Joe's (convenient because the TJ's has a sub-par produce selection). Also a great place to pick up a smoothie!

People's Food Co-op *3029 SE 21st. Ave. / 503-232-9051 / Open daily 9a-9p* Their slogan, "Food for People, Not Profit" says it all. Free of all meat products (including rennet). People's is the best place to buy food in the southeast if you are hesitant (or unwilling) to support large chain stores. They have a beautiful selection of local organic produce and a well-stocked bulk section. The prices tend to be a few cents more than those at the bigger shops in town, but the community atmosphere and environmentally conscious attitude of People's make shopping there worth it

Sheridan Fruit Company *408 SE 3rd Ave. (at SE MLK) / 503-236-2114 / Mo-Sa 6a-8p, Su 6a-6p* Local produce distributor that acts also as a neighborhood grocer. Pick up low-priced fruits and veggies here (organics and locally-grown stuff, too!). Sheridan has a great bulk foods and beer selection as well. Gourmet foods and a meat counter too! And it's the only place I can find Sclafani products in this burg (just like home!) (sg)

(dm)

Theaters

Avalon/Wunderland *3532 SE Belmont St. / 503-238-1617* Come and play Dance Dance Revolution at the nickel arcade! Take in a dollar movie in their busted seats and enjoy cheap popcorn! Granted, not all of the games are a nickel (some cost several nickels, in fact), you can definitely have a great time in Avalon for a couple of dollars. They have classic games as well as new favorites. You can also play skee-ball and trade your tickets in for obnoxious prizes like disappearing ink! (ng)

Bagdad Theater and Pub *3702 SE Hawthorne Blvd. / 503- 232-6676 / Su-Th 11a-12a, Fr-Sa 11a-1a* Ah, what's not to like about the Bagdad? It's been a landmark on Hawthorne for three-quarters of a century, always a focal point and source of pride for the neighborhood. Universal Pictures built the Bagdad in 1927 for the then-enormous sum of $100,000 to make this opulent movie and vaudeville palace. It's Middle-Eastern meets California Deco architecture is appealing then as it is now. It retained the live vaudeville productions through the 1940's, and then converted to its current all-movie format. The Bagdad trudged through the mid-century with its one screen format, until 1979 when it was converted into a tri-plex. In 1974, the original backstage area was converted into a screening room called, cleverly enough, the Backstage, which showed mostly B-movies. In 1975 the Bagdad was the chosen theater for the Oregon premiere of One Flew Over the Cuckoo's Nest, the movie based off of Oregon native Ken Kesey's novel. Actors Jack Nicholson and Louise Fletcher, and producer Michael Douglas were on hand. In 1991, the theater was purchased by those ever-enterprising McMenamin Brothers, who renovated the "grand dame of Hawthorne" and made it the brewpub-and-second-run-film format that we currently know and love. During the renovation period in 1991 the Bagdad saw yet another Hollywood premiere, this time My Own Private Idaho, the feature directed by Portlandite Gus Van Sant and starring River Phoenix (RIP) and Keanu Reaves. More recently the likes of Sean Penn and Dennis Kucinich were seen in front of the ol' Bagdad. Seventy-nine years old and still attracting stars! (sg)

Cinemagic *2021 SE Hawthorne Blvd. / 503-231-7919* Second run movies for cheap(er).

Clinton St. Theater *2522 SE Clinton St / 503-238-8899 / $6 for regular shows, $4 for matinees and Tuesdays* Opening in 1915, the Clinton is the oldest operating theater in Portland, one of the oldest in existence in the US, and possibly the oldest continuously operating theater west of the Mississippi. And the Clinton has had the Rocky Horror Picture Show playing every Saturday night for almost thirty years! One thing, though, is the Clinton couldn't make up it's mind on what it wanted to be called. Originally the Clinton, it changed to the less-distinctive 26th Avenue Theatre in 1945, then to the not-much-better Encore in 1969. Finally in 1976 it reverted back to the name we know and love. The Clinton has made its name in recent years for showing arthouse films and having interesting themed movie fests, like Stag Film Festival and Dog Day, most notably (the latter inviting dogs to watch movies like Rin Tin Tin, Tippy the Wonder-Pup and more!) Now the Clinton has an adjoining brewpub (the smallest in Portland) so you can enjoy some fine beer with your movie! The outside of the Clinton is a bit deceiving, as the building itself is non-descript and the Clinton lacks the spectacular marquee setup that some other PDX cinemas enjoy. But once inside it's pure movie magic! (sg)

(aro)

(aro)

Thrift Stores

Avant Garden Vintage Thrift *2853 SE Stark* More on the vintage side than usual junk-shop thrift, but prices are equitable and there's a wide assortment of styles and eras to choose from, in clothing and home decór. The well-traveled proprietor has a number of odds and ends from her trips abroad, including Asian movie posters. Just ask and she can provide you with summaries of the film plots! Strangest of all are the vintage Chairman Mao alarm clocks. Avant Garden provides free pickup of donations. (en)

Useful Resources

FREE GEEK *1731 SE 10th Ave. / 503-232-9350 / Tu-Sa 11:00a-7:00p* The lifespan of the average new computer is measured in months, not years. The vast majority of these "old", unwanted computers end up in landfills or are shipped overseas, where the parts poison the people and the land. FREE GEEK is a non-profit who aims to stop this while at the same time arming underprivileged folks with computers. They collect, assess, reuse and recycle computer hardware that individuals and organizations donate to them, rather than dumping as trash. The hardware is sorted and tested by volunteers who both help the cause and learn about computers at the same time. All parts that can be reused, are, and those which cannot are responsibly sold as scrap or recycled. In the end, the volunteers' time is traded in for their own computer, which they conveniently learned all about during the process! Additionally, FREE GEEK has classes, all sorts of outreach programs, sells or donates hardware to non-profits, and has a thrift store open to the public. Plus so much more. (jv)

Video Stores

Beverly Hills Video II   *7475 SE 72nd Ave / (503) 777-2626*

Clinton St Video   *2501 SE Clinton St. / 503-236-9030* Great selection of cult, indie, and foreign films.

Movie Madness and More   *4320 SE Belmont St. / 503-234-436* Huge amount of videos and DVDs for your viewing pleasure. Most videos: $2; new releases: $2.75; employee picks $1. Specializing in the hard to find (documentary, foreign, cult and animation), but also a good selection of mainstream too. And the store is like a mini movie museum, as memorabilia from movies past and present fill the place. There's also something refreshing about the makeshiftness and collagesqueness of the store, a nice change if you're used to the stiflingly boring mainstream movie rental places. (sl)

Videorama (Ladds Circle)   *1990 SE Ladds / (503)231-1181 / Mon-Sun 12pm-10pm*

(aro)

Southwest / Northwest

Southwest

Art Supplies

Art Media   *902 SW Yamhill St. / 503-223-3724 / 9a-6.30p Mo-Sa, Su 12p-5*   Portland's locally owned source for your art supplies. Good selection of stuff (with a separate paper room). A bit pricy with some hidden bargains.

Bars

Kelly's Olympian   *426 SW Washington / 503-228-3669 / Open 9am - 2:30am*   Motorcycle-centric downtown bar with $1 PBRs Sunday-Wednesday all night. Surprisingly kick-ass breakfast and bar food and extremely friendly staff. (nb)

Tugboat Brewing Co.   *711 SW Ankeny / 503-226-2508*   This small brewpub hidden on "Ankeny Alley" (in the same block as the much more famous Mary's Club) serves up tasty, unpretentious beers for cheap! You'll never pay more than $3 for a pint of house beer, and there's plenty of opportunities to even get that pint for $2 (happy hour, nightly specials). The interior is cozy in the good sense of the word, and it's one of the few places in town to see experimental/free jazz on a regular basis. (sg)

Books, Zines, Comix and the like

Annie Blooms Books   *7834 SW Capitol Hwy / 503-246-0053 / 9a-10p daily*   A gem of a bookstore tucked away in cozy Multnomah Village. Annie Bloom's offers a great selection of stuff, including many independently published books. They also host readings and other events regularly. (sg)

Counter Media   *927 SW Oak St. / 503-226-8141*   A densely packed, two-room bookstore along the Oak Street block (next to Half & Half and Reading Frenzy). One room has a fine selection of vintage and new porn, er, "erotica", and the other half houses hard-to-find pop culture books and memorabilia, as well as a thoughtfully stocked assortment of indie, rare & foreign comics. (nb)

Looking Glass Book Store   *7983 SE 13th Ave / 503-227-4760*   Despite being one of the oldest independent bookstore in town (in biz since the early '70s when it was a bastion of radical literature), for some reason Looking Glass is not well known. Is it because it was in a hidden corner of downtown? Or that it was too close to Borders? That should change now that it moved to the Sellwood neighborhood, an area lacking a book seller. You'll find inside a good selection of lit and a helpful staff that will give you the attention you can't get at McBorders. And there's always an interesting event or reading going on. Support your independent bookstore! (sg)

Reading Frenzy   *921 SW Oak St. / 503-274-1449 / Mo-Sa 11a-7p, Su 12p-6*   The zine mecca of the Pacific Northwest! A great place to browse, purchase, and bump into all those Portland zinesters collecting their consignments. (Yes, Reading Frenzy accepts zines for consignment.) The Frenzy also sells crafty goods and the like from local peeps and cool stuff from around the world. Readings, signings, and other events occur here throughout the year. Its selection of current alternative and mini comics is hands-down the best in town! Make sure to check out the IPRC (see separate listing) when you're here, because no zine-related visit to Portland is complete without visiting Reading Frenzy and the IPRC.

Coffeehouses, Teahouses and the like

Fehrenbacher Hof Coffee House *1125 SW 19th Ave / 503-223-4493 / Mo-Fr 6a-6p, Sa-Su 8a-4p* This is one of my favorite "hidden" coffeehouses in town. Tucked away in a corner not normally travelled to by the "hip" crowd (that'd be Goose Hollow), the Fehrenbacher serves up some great caffeinated beverages. And they always seem to have delicious baked goods at prices that can't be beat. The back room is a cozy place to while away a drizzly Northwestern afternoon, contentedly reading or drawing without worrying about running into someone you know (which can happen regularly at other places). And the Fehrenhacher is owned by everyone's favorite eccentric ex-mayor, Bud Clark. Whoop Whoop! (sg)

Reading Frenzy (nb)

(cc)

Half & Half   *923 SW Oak St. / 503-222-4495 / Mo-Fr 8a-6p, Sa 10a-6p, Su 12p-5* A great early morning coffee & donut stop, or tasty sandwiches & soup for lunch. Here is also the place to buy your sundries: Chairman Mao pins, rain caps, EmergenC, tampons, tricks and safety pins. Owned and operated by very cool people. Free wifi via IPRC. (rg)

Stumptown Coffee Roasters (Downtown)   *128 SW 3rd Ave at Ash / 503-295-6144 / Mo-Th 7a-9p, 7a-11p Fr-Sa, 8a-5p Su* Also serves wine and beer.

Donuts

Voodoo Doughnuts   *22 SW Third Av. / 503-241-4704 / 10p-10a Mo-Th, Fr even 10p-3a, Sat 10p-3a, closed Su, Mon morn 6a-10* Sorry, Portland's Dunkin' Donuts (how few and crappy they were) are all closed, and the Krispy Kremes are out in exotic suburbia (Clackamas?) Where are native East Coasters going to get their donut jones, especially late at night? Fortunately, there's one beacon of hope in the donut darkness of PDX, and that is Voodoo Doughnuts. This shop specializes only in overnight donuts. Located between Theatre Paris and Berbatti's, this place is literally a hole-in-the-wall, complete with Portland's Smallest Stage (live music every Wednesday). And the donuts are good – they even have vegan ones! Specialties include the eponymous Voodoo Donut, topped with chocolate, filled with jelly ("blood") and poked through with a pretzel; also worth noting are the various fritters, the Tex-Ass Donut (can you eat it?) and a donut shaped like a penis filled with creme – yes, we are being dead serious here. In the last few years, Voodoo has become a Portland institution, featured in many different media all around the world, and the owners ran for City Council (again!) Mark our words: no visit to Portland is complete without stopping here! (sg)

(hq)

Ever-nebulous "Other" Category

Portland Saturday Market

108 W Burnside St. / 503-222-607
Located under the west side the Burnside Bridge, Saturday market is the largest continually operating open-air crafts market in the United States, since 1974. Open Sundays in summer too. This is a good place to drop off your mom for a few hours when she's visiting town.

Late Night Eats

The Roxy *1121 SW Stark St / 503-223-9160 / open 24 hours Tu-Su, closed Mo* Yer typical greasy-diner fare. Quite a lively hangout later in the evening.

Museums

Oregon Maritime Museum *Aboard the Stern-Wheel Steamboat docked off Waterfront Park/NW Front Ave between Morrison & Burnside Bridge / 503-224-7724 / Wed – Sun 11 – 4 pm* Ship models, paintings, and more. And most importantly, patient volunteers will answer questions as you wander around the ship and engine rooms. $3 – 5, Group $2 per person (cb)

Wells Fargo Museum – Portland *1300 SW Fifth Avenue (in the Wells Fargo Center Tower) / 503-886-1102 / M – F, 9 am – 6 pm* Try out the Morse code with a friend on telegraph stations wired on opposite sides of the lobby. Also see displays on banking in Oregon, the stagecoach line from California, and riverboats of gold on the Columbia River. Near the elevators you'll find a miniature model of the Portlandia statue (cb)

Other Mercantile-type Operations

Council Thrift Shop *1127 SW Morrison St. / -get- / M-F 10-6, Sat 10-5* Seemingly small from the outside, Council Thrift stretches back into three good-sized rooms packed with oddball goods. The clothing selection is decent, and toys have a room all to themselves. A flyer on the door mentions any special discounts. It's right on the #15 bus line too!

Finnegan's Toys *922 SW Yamhill St. / 503-221-0306* Upscale educational toy store that you will dig. Look here for neoprints and Sanrio merchandise.

Pioneer Square (dw)

Parks

Council Crest Park *SW Council Crest Dr.* This hill is the highest point in the city at 1,073 feet (327 meters). Back in the day (1907-1929) there was an amusement park here (similar to Oaks Park, which still survives) but unfortunately, not anymore. Instead, we now have a great vantage point where you can see five snow-capped peaks (St. Helens, Rainier, Adams, Jefferson, and Hood) and 3,000 square miles of land and rivers , plus the city itself. Of course, that it's if it's sunny out. Access from SW Greenway Ave. (sg)

Gabriel Park *SW 45 Av & SW Vermont St* This large park situated on the edge of Multnomah Village has plenty of park things like ball courts and dog off-leash areas. Running through the middle of the park is a creek with wooded natural areas surrounding it. (I wish some Eastside parks had this...) If you find yourself out this way, Gabriel Park is a to-do. (sg)

Hoyt Arboretum *4000 SW Fairview Blvd / (503) 228-TREE* A tree-hugger's paradise! This is a 214 acre "tree museum" on the western tip of Washington Park. 4,300 different trees and over 800 types of shrubs are on display here. The Arboretum has the largest collection of coniferous (boreal) trees anywhere in the world. The collection includes rare trees, like the long-thought-to-be-extinct Dawn Redwood from China, plus traditional west-coast team-players Giant Sequoias, Coast Redwoods, and Douglas Firs. Learn about our friends the trees whilst romping through a hipster-free environment. (sg)

Ira Keller (Forecourt) Fountain *SW Clay St at SW Third Ave* During Portland's urban renewal era in the mid 1950's to early 1970's, this parcel of land across from Civic

Auditorium had been acquired by the city for a park. Designed by Angela Danadjieva in 1968 and completed in 1970, the multi-tiered, modernist-designed fountain became an instant hit in town and abroad. (It also atracted "the hippies", which didn't please City Councillors like Frank Ivancie.) In 1978, Forecourt Fountain was renamed for Ira Keller, former director of the Portland Development Commission (1958-72) the personality most responsible (besides former Mayor Terry Schrunk 1957-73) for urban renewal in Portland. Keller knew how to get his way, and projects like South Auditorium and Memorial Coliseum reflect that. Reflect on that as you stare into the recirculating waters. Or take a dip on a hot day! (sg)

The Park Blocks   *North: along NW Park between W Burnside and NW Glisan – South: along SW Park between SW Salmon and Portland State University* Back in the northeast, they would call this a "green". These elm-lined parks are a great place to take a leisurely stroll and to have a picnic lunch amongst the hustle and bustle of downtown.

Pioneer Square.   *Bounded by SW Morrison St, SW Broadway, SW Yamhill, and SW 6th Ave* The city's boosters like to refer to this as the "living room of Portland". Originally the site of the Portland Hotel, grandest of all hotels in the city, the hostelry was torn down in 1951 to make way for a ... parking lot. Eventually, someone had the idea that the space would be better utilized for a more public use, so Pioneer Square was created in the '80s. It's the central meeting place of town, done in a European manner. This is probably the best place for people watching in town! Both the bus transit mall and Max lines intersect here.

Waterfront Park (cc)

Salmon St. Spring. *SW Front and SW Salmon* Crazy kids (and the young at heart) ride their bikes through the center of this fountain. It's like running through sprinklers.

Terwilliger Parkway and Bike Lanes This linear park stretches a couple miles along SW Terwilliger Blvd. From SW Barbur Blvd. Northward to almost I-405. The street has bike lanes in both directions, making this a great place to ride, although there are quite a few hills. The best part of the ride is the great (and somewhat secret) views you'll get of the city below, especially in winter when the trees are bare.

Tryon Creek State Park A bit off the beaten path, but worth noting. This nature park is situated in a valley along Tyron Creek, one of the last free-flowing streams to be found in Portland. Fourteen miles of trail meander through the park's forested slopes, including a paved all-abilities access trail, an equestrian trail, and a bike path that parallels Terwilliger Blvd. (If you ever need to get to--shudder--Lake Oswego on bike, this path is gonna be your best bet.) There's also a nature center located at 11321 SW Terwilliger Blvd if you're into that. (sg)

Washington Park. This park is probably the city's most popular (i.e. touristy). From it, you get some spectacular views of the city. Contained within its boundaries are Hoyt Arboretum, the Japanese Garden, Children's Museum, the world-renowned International Rose Test Gardens, and, for better or worse, the World Forestry Center and Portland Zoo. Only the Rose Garden and Arboretum are free, get out the wallet for the other attractions! Expect two things of this park: large crowds, especially on weekends and doubly-especially in the summer; and when you're parents visit, they'll want to go here. One way to access the park is from the MAX line's Zoo Station – this stop is the only underground station on the system – where Zoombomb starts (see listing under "Bicycles"). The easiest access is from SW Park Place West of SW Vista..

Waterfront Park. This linear greenway lies along the west bank of the Willamette River between the Steel and Hawthorne Bridges. Ages ago, the waterfront was filled with warehouses that housed freight from the ships that plied the river. After World War II, the commercial buildings on the riverbanks were torn down to make way for Harbor Drive, an ugly monstrosity of a freeway. Downtown was effectively cut off from the river. But not everyone was happy, and in the early 70's, the city tore down the freeway to make room for this park. Progress, indeed! Now you can leisurely stroll the banks of the river and watch the boats go by. During the summer it seems there is a festival here every week.

The Wildwood Trail A 30 mile nature trail connecting several westside parks running along the spine of the west hills. It begins near the Oregon Zoo at Washington Park, heads north to Hoyt Arboretum and Pittock Mansion, and finally terminates at the north end of Forest Park.

Willamette Park and the West Bank bike path This park (off SW Macadam) is great for river views. If you somehow have a canoe or other watercraft, you could launch it here. There is a paved multi-use path that runs through the park, connecting it to the Sellwood Bridge and the SW Industrial district. This trail is less "natural" than the OMSI-Springwater path on the east bank, as it passes through several apartment and business complexes (and can get quite choked with traffic at times). To access the trail is a bit tricky; the best way from downtown is to take the Waterfront Path south of the Hawthorne Bridge through the condominium nonsense and under the Marquam Bridge. Then continue on SW Moody Ave through the new highrise construction and find the trailhead near an espresso stand.

Pizza

Hot Lips Pizza (PSU) *1901 SW 6th Ave / 503-224-0311 / Mo-Sa 11a-9:30p, Su 12a-8p* While the pizza at Hot Lips is good, a nice approximation of East Coast Style, what makes this joint stand out is its standards. Hot lips uses locally grown, organic ingredients. Hot Lips has made a commitment to reduce its impact on the environment, even it means less profits. Their goal is to become a sustainable company. For those of the vegan persuasion, there are options, whether it be their foccacia, or a tasty vegan slice (not made daily, though). There are two locations in the downtown area: near the PSU campus, and in the Pearl District by the main post office at 721 NW 10th Ave. 503-595-234 (sg)

Rocco's Pizza *949 SW Oak St. / 503-223-9835* Ah, the punk-rock pizza slice: an ungodly mound of cheese on bland crust which will conquer the nastiest of coffeeguts, followed by hours of mindless, drooling digestion. Longtime downtown fixture across

Jackpot Records (cc)

Downtown food carts (dw)

from Powell's. The big draw to Rocco's is how BIG their pizza is. The question is, can you handle it? Open late on Friday/Saturday. (nb)

Record Stores

2nd Ave Records   *400 SW 2nd Ave. / 503-222-3783* Another Portland record store hidden away in a crevice of downtown. Here the emphasis is on the hip-hop, punk, and t-shirts, and a supposedly good selection of ska.

Jackpot Records (Indie Rock Block)   *203 SW 9th Av (at W Burnside) / 503-222-0990*

Restaurants

Berbatis/Berbati's Pan   *10 SW 3rd Ave. / 503-248-4579* Greek restaurant, bar, and show venue. Check out their happy hour menu since regular dinner is pretty spendy.

Divine Café   *SW 9th Ave between Washington and Alder.* Veggie/vegan cart with lots of good food and outside seating.

Dreamer's Café   *SW 5th Av between Stark and Oak on / Mo-Fr 11a-6p* A problem with being vegetarian/vegan is that it's hard to find good comfort food. Oh sure, you can go to a lot of places and get "thai tofu something" but that's all so...healthy. What about somethng that'll stick to your ribs? Dreamer's serves up tasty sandwiches that imitate their meaty counterparts. You can get a scrumptious "not steak" sandwich done up with mushrooms, or a "not meatball" sub of chickpeas and plenty of sauce. And when you order the meatball sub, the guy will say "Meatball Parm, right", indicating yes indeed this is in an East Coast vein. You can get french fries with your order, which can be hard to find in the land of foodcarts. (sg)

El Grillo   *703 SW Ankeny St (at Broadway) / 503-241-0462* Good, cheap Mexican food (bean & cheese burrito $2.75!) open to midnight most nights. This place seems to be downtown's best-kept secret. It's connected to Mary's Club, the infamous "live nude revue", so if you need to use the bathroom, you have to go through through a strip club(!)

Koji's Osakaya   *606 SW Broadway / (503) 294-1169* At moderate prices, Koji's delivers quality noodles and sushi. Gigantic bowls of homemade ramen, perfect miso soup, and your typical sushi fare. Chicken Donburi was unappetizing -- beware. The northeast location seems much cleaner and the food fresher than downtown. (nb)

Veganopolis Caféteria   *412 SW 4th Ave / 503-226-3400 / 8a-6p Mo-Sa* Brand new vegan eatery serving up breakfast and lunch fare. Breakfast is buffet style, $5.50/lb. Lunch is a smattering of sandwiches, soups, and specials. (sg)

Theaters

Whitsell Auditorium   *1219 SW Park Ave. in the Portland Art Museum / 503-221-115* The Northwest Film Center shows movies here. They are often artsy, foreign films

Thrift Stores

Council Thrift Shop   *1127 SW Morrison / M-F 10-6, Sat 10-5* Seemingly small from the outside, Council Thrift stretches back into three good-sized rooms packed with odd-ball goods. The clothing selection is decent, and toys have a room all to themselves. A flyer on the door mentions any special discounts. Ités right on the #15 bus line too! (en)

Useful Resources

Independent Publishing Resource Center (IPRC)   *917 SW Oak St, Suite 218 / 503-827-0249 / Mo 12p-10p, Tu-Th 4p-10p, Fr-Su 12p-6* The IPRC, short for Independent Publishing Resource Center, is located upstairs from Reading Frenzy in the North Pacific Bldg. The IPRC facilitates creative expression and identity by providing individual access to the resources and tools for the creation of independently published media and art. They are a non profit resource center which includes a zine lending library (with library cards available to all), zine workspace and supplies, and a computer lab. Other things available are a copier, book binding supplies, letterpresses, a mimeograph machine, art gallery, and more. Workshops on various aspects of independent publishing and DIY art are available. The IPRC is open to members (sliding scale yearly membership starting at $40) and to non-members (for a small hourly fee). Make sure to check out Reading Frenzy (see separate listing) when you're here, because no zine-related visit to Portland is complete without visiting Reading Frenzy and the IPRC!!!

IPRC (ar)

Outside In *1132 SW 13th Ave. / 503-535-3800 / (medical appointments call 503-223-4121)* Outside In is a social service agency dedicated to serving low-income adults and homeless youth. Current programs include a community health clinic that provides very-low-cost sliding-scale pay service, a homeless youth program designed to help homeless youth obtain independent living, and risk education.   Outside In is a great place to go if you need non-emergency medical treatment and have no money. The only drawback is you have to be under 30 to use the traditional medical clinic. (They provide naturopathic doctors and interns, acupuncturists and Chinese herbalists that are available for people of all ages, however.) Clinic hours are Mon-Fri, see their website or call to find out what their hours are, as it varies daily depending on the service.

(sl)

Northwest

Art Supplies

Utrecht Art Supply *1122 NW Everett St. / 503-417-8024 / Mo-Fr 9a-p, Sa 9a-6p,
Su 11a-5* National chain art supply store with decent prices, ample selection, and
disaffected staff. Watch out, though, they'll try to get you to get one of those "cards".
Don't do it!

Books, Zines, Comix and the like

Floating World Comics *20 NW 5th Ave, Suite 101 / 503-241-0227 / Tu-Su 11a-7p*
This place has an amazing selection of comics from the smallest and most elite of small
presses. Also, zines, an exotic selection of pricey art books, and a friendly knowledgeable
owner. (bla)

 The Powell's Empire *1005 W Burnside / 503-228-4651 800-878-7323 / open daily
365 days a year 9a-11p* The largest independent bookstore in the entire world! No matter how you slice it, it's a booklover's dream, with extensive selections of new and used
books. The main store (City of Books) takes up an entire city block (and four floors) and
requires a map to navigate it.

Powell's Technical Books *33 NW Park Ave. at NW Couch / 503-228-3906 / Mo-Sa
9a-9p, Su 11a-7* Technical books -- go figure. For all you tech geeks out there.

Powell's (ks)

Chain Grocery Stores, Supermarkets, etc.

Trader Joe's (Northwest) *2122 NW Glisan St / 971-544-0788*

Whole Foods *1210 NW Couch St (at Burnside) / 503-525-434 / Daily 8a-10p* A Texas based natural-gourmet grocery chain (and arch-rival to Wild Oats). The food prices are a bit steep, but there are samples and vegan donuts. Super-convenient if you're downtown.

Fred Meyer (Stadium) *100 NW 20th Pl / 503-273-2004 / 7a-11p daily* This is the Freddie's Jello Biafra referred to.

Coffeehouses, Teahouses and the like

Anna Bannanas *1214 NW 21st Ave. / 503-274-2559 / Mo-Th 7:30a-11p, Fr 7.30a-12a, Sa 8a-12a, Su 8a-11* Commonly referred to as "the other good coffee house" in the Northwest neighborhood, Anna Bannana's is in an old foursquare house, meaning it feels more homey than a standard coffee joint. The staff is friendly and the coffee is good... what more could you want?

Coffee Time *712 Nw 21st St. / (503) 497-1090* Northwest Portland's infamous late-night coffeehouse (usually open til 3am). Rare is the moment you'll find this place empty of people, as this place is an epicenter of "cool" kids, armchair philosophers, artists, chess players, and the Ambercrombie set. Their coffee prices are a bit steep. Either people really like Coffee Time or really don't like Coffee Time, so be forewarned! Free wifi.

TeaZone *510 NW 11th Ave. / 503-221-2130 / Mo-We 8a-6p, Th-Fr 8a-8p, Sa 10a-8p, Su 10a-6* European style tea salon with a good selection of teas, plus those neat bubble tea drinks with tapioca in them.

World Cup Coffee and Tea (Northwest neighborhood) *1740 NW Glisan St / 503.228.4152 / 6:30 AM to 8:00 PM Mo-Fr, 7:00 AM to 7:00 PM Sa-Su* This local coffee roaster specializes in fair trade, organic, shade-grown coffee. Originally just a roaster, they now have three cafés to quench your coffee thirst. Chill in the Glisan St store for a lazy Sunday afternoon of sketching while waiting to catch a show at the Mission. Rub shoulders with the new bourgeoise in the Pearl District-Ecotrust Building (NW 9th) store and then go play in the water at Jameson Square. For ultimate people watching (and book reading), fight the crowds for an empty seat at the Powell's on Burnside location. And drink good coffee at all three! (sg)

World Cup Coffee and Tea (Ecotrust Bldg in the Pearl) *721 NW 9th Av / 503.546.7377 / 6:30 AM to 7:00 PM Mo-Fr, 7:30 AM to 7:00 PM Sa-Su*

World Cup Coffee and Tea (Powells Downtown) *1005 W Burnside St / 503.228.4651x234 / 9:00 AM - 11:00 PM every day of the year*

Backspace (ecd)

Ever-nebulous "Other" Category

Backspace *115 NW 5th Ave. / 503-248-2900 / Mon-Fri 7am-2am, Saturday 10am-2am, Sunday 12pm-12am* Huge art gallery, coffeehouse, and retrocade with a focus on a large central hub of network gaming PCs wired to a constant slew of vidheads battling it out. Comfortable atmosphere with Stumptown coffee, baked goods, free wifi, a monthly rotation of surprisingly good art, and two ubergeek gaming conference rooms with projection-screen XBox, Gamecube, PS2 and Atari 2600 (!). (nb)

Hostels

Hostelling International-Portland, Northwest Neighborhood. *425 NW 18th Av / 503-241-2783 / Office hours: 8am-11pm daily* Portland's most centrally located hostel, located in the heart of the Northwest Neighborhood. The hostel is housed in a restored turn-of-the-century historic building and has an on-site coffee bar. Free pastries and bread. Kitchen, lockers, laundry, and Internet are available. Helpful and friendly staff and great information on things to see and do. Dorm rate: $17-22 (higher rates in summer), private room rate: $36-69 (depending on room and season), plus lodging tax and a $3 fee for non-Hostelling International members. Open all year with 24-hour access. Reservations are advisable during the summer. Reservations accepted by phone, mail, fax, and e-mail. (sg)

Museums

Oregon Jewish Museum *310 NW Davis St / 503-226-3600 / Tues – Friday 11 – 2 pm, Sun 1 – 4* Only museum in the Pacific Northwest dedicated to preserving and exhibiting Jewish art, history, & culture. Located in Old Town, a neighborhood with long-standing Jewish Roots. $3 suggested donation. (cb)

Oregon Nikkei Legacy Center *121 NW 2nd Ave / 503-224-1458 / T – Sat 11 – 3 pm, Sun Noon – 3 pm* This Japanese-American history museum and center has an amazing model of Oldtown showing how the area where the museum sits today was the center of Portland's Japantown. The museum explores what happened to the Japanese-Americans who were forced to move to camps after the Pearl Harbor WWII bombing. A very powerful experience. $3 suggested donation. (cb)

The Shanghai Tunnels of Portland *Tours Depart from Hobo's Restaurant, 120 NW 3rd Av / 503-622-4798 / Fri and Sat* Not quite a museum, but this experience is full of artifacts, dark tunnels, and story telling that will transport you back to the early days of Portland, say 1890s. When after a drink in the tavern, you could wake up on a ship heading out into the Pacific Ocean. "Shanghaiing" involved drugged drinks, trap doors, and tunnels to the Willamette. It was a way to get cheap labor up until 1915. Call for Tour Schedule. Most Friday and Saturdays, $12 Adult, $7 children (cb)

Other Mercantile-type Operations

Ground Kontrol *511 NW Couch St / 503-796-9364 / Su-Th 12p-10p, Fri-Sa noon-midnight, 21 and over all nights after 7pm* The only retrocade in the Northwest. They also buy and sell old video game systems, and now they sell beer! So if you're looking for an Atari 2600 with that pint of PBR, come here.

Parks

Forest Park *NW 29 & Upshur to Newberry Rd* A 5,000 acre wilderness preserve located in the hills (Tualatin Mountains) of Northwest Portland, Forest Park is America's largest forested urban wilderness. Over 70 miles of trails and fire lanes guarantees that you can spend days here exploring the wonders of the outdoors. While all the paths are hike-able,(there is a handicap-accessible trail at the Lower Macleay Trailhead, 2960 NW Upshur) only on the Leif Erickson trail (and some firelanes) are you legally allowed to ride a bicycle. (Mountain bikes are best suited for this route.) It's one of those places that, once you're inside surrounded by towering Doug Firs, you'll say to yourself, "I can't believe I'm still in a city!" (And dude, you are!) If there's a "Top Ten Reasons Why To Live in Portland" list, I'm sure Forest Park would be on it. (Maybe I should write one...) There are several ways to enter the park but the easier options are either via the Wildwood Trail (see separate entry), the Leif Erickson Trailhead at NW Thurman St. west of NW 31st Ave, or the Balch Creek Trailhead at NW Upshur St and NW 28th Ave (sg)

(dm)

Pittock Mansion and Park. A big fancy-ass house built by former Oregonian pub-
lisher Henry L. Pittock back in the early twentieth century. Now it is part of our wonderful
park system. They give tours of the mansion daily (which cost money) if you're into that.
But if not, come up here to check out the great views, maybe even bring a picnic lunch to
liven up the event.. C'mon, an eccentric millionaire is going to build his "castle" on one
of the best view-points in the city, right? Access at 3229 NW Pittock Dr, off W Burnside.
Bicyclists take note: big steep hills to get here!

Performance and Art Spaces

Just Be Toys/Compound *107 NW 5th Ave. / 503-796-2733* This business is a
combination of two different things. The ground floor is Just Be Toys, featuring many
cool Japanese toys, products, and media. The upstairs is Compound, an art gallery featuring urban influenced, graf-style, or Japanese art, which changes every First Thursday
(see artwalk listing)

Motel *19 NW 5th Ave, Suite C, storefront on NW Couch between 5th and 6th / 503-
222-6699 / Tu-Su 12p-6p* This new boutique sells hand-crafted goodness made by local
artists (some of which even do zines!) Plus they have a gallery space which features
new art every First Thursday (see artwalk listing) (sg)

Pizza

Escape from New York Pizzeria *622 NW 23rd Ave. / 503-227-5423 / 11:30a-11p daily* Usually, when a pizzeria bills itself "New York Style", they overdecorate the place with Big Apple paraphernalia (for "authenticity") to hide the fact that they have no effing clue as to what "New York Style" is. While Escape has the NYC décor in spades, don't let that fool you. They know their shit (excuse my french). The crust is of perfect thickness, and there's the correct balance of sauce and cheese. If you want a slice, there are only three choices-cheese, pepperoni, and the special. If you're into gourmet pizza with fancy ingredients, try Pizzicato. But if you want great pizza from an establishment owned by real New Yorkers, then come here! Tip: bring your East Coast pals here if they constantly moan, "there's no good pizza on the West Coast."

Hot Lips Pizza (Pearl) *721 NW 9th Av / 503-595-2342 / Mo-Th 11a-9p, Fr-Sa 11a-10p, Su 12p-8p*

Tribute's Pizza *2272 NW Kearney St. / 503-299-1200 / 11a-9p Su-Th, 11a-10p Fr-S* Yet another pie-maker doing it in the NYC vein. Originally called "Richie B's" (you can't get more east-coast than that!), the name changed to reflect that Mr. B, an authentic Noo Yawker, left the biz. But the quality pizzas he brought here are still being made. While very close to Escape, this shop doesn't enjoy the same popularity. But that means you don't have to wait in line as long! And Tribute's offers subs (or can we say grinders?) which is a rarity in PDX's pizzerias.

Record Stores

Everyday Music *1313 W Burnside St / 503-274-0961* Extensive selection of new and used compact discs and LPs. Check out the recent arrivals for an occasional gem. Open 9am to midnight seven days a week, 365 days a year.

Music Millenium (Westside) *801 NW 23rd Av / 503-248-0163 / 10a-10p Mo-Sa, 11a-9p*

Restaurants

Mio Sushi *2271 NW Johnson St. / 503-221-146* Relatively cheap sushi in an unpretentious atmosphere. Good veggie menu

Pearl Bakery *102 NW 9th Ave. / 503-827-0910 / Mo-Fr 6a-6p, Sa 7a-5* Sweet-ass sweets that you will dig, yo. You can't go wrong with their desserty treats. Featuring breads referred to as "artisan"

Sisters of the Road Café *133 NW 6th Ave. / 503-222-5694* Super cheap café, designed to serve low-income folks, where you can work in exchange for food. Also accepts food stamps.

Vegetarian House *22 NW 4th Av / 503-274-0160 / Mo-Fr 11a-2:30p, 4:30p-9p, Sa-Su 11a-9p* For some reason, finding a strictly veggie Asian restaurant is hard in

(ks)

Portland. But each year it gets a bit easier. Vegetarian House is a no-meat Chinese restaurant located in, of all places, Chinatown. (Just beyond the gate!) The House knows
how to make a mean faux-meat. And if you are unsure of what to get (since everything
sounds good on the menu), come to the weekday lunch buffet. All you can eat for $5.99!
And the House is run by followers of the "Spiritual Master"!

Small Grocery Stores

Food Front *2375 NW Thurman St. / 503-222-5658 / Open daily 8a-9p* Natural food
co-op type market found in the border zone where "Nob Hill" meets the Northwest Industrial District. Good place to pick up your organic produce and bulk food items. Their deli
makes a swell lunch too.

Theaters

Cinema 21 *616 NW 21st Ave. / 503-223-4515* The northwest neighborhood's inde-
pendently-owned, first-run art house theater. Regularly shows indie flicks you won't find
elsewhere. $7 admission, $6 student/matinee, and $4 for first shows Sat-Sun.

Mission Theater and Pub *1624 NW Glisan St. / 503-223-452* Talk about history!
First, way back in the early 1890's, what is now the Mission Theater was a church for the
Swedish Evangelical Mission, where missionaries planned pilgrimages to Asia. Then
the church moved on, and the Mission became a Longshoreman's Hall. Finally, in 1987

McMenamins renovated the space to its current use: cheap movies and beer! Viva cheap movies!

Thrift Stores

William Temple House Thrift Store *2230 NW Glisan Street / M-Th & Sat 10-6, Fri 10-8, Sun 12-6* Located just off the NW 23rd Street upscale shopping area, this place is quite unsnooty and chock-full of useful and/or frivolous gear. The range of household décor is especially good, compared even to the Goodwill store at 2215 W Burnside. Be sure to look in the display areas at the checkout counter for even more wacky stuff. Clothing variety is reasonable but the racks are chaotic and crowded together. This store has occasional bag sales as well. (en)

Video Stores

Videorama (Pearl Dist) *1136 NW Lovejoy / (503)796-2825 / Mon-Sun 12pm-10pm*

Paul Bunyan statue in Kenton (North Portland) (sg)

Outer North
Coffeehouses, Teahouses and the like

North Star Coffeehouse   *7540 N Interstate Av (at the Lombard MAX stop) / (503) 285-5800* The name probably alludes to the location of this coffee joint--in Kenton just north of Lombard in NoPo (which is almost four miles north of Burnside, as the crow flies). In an area not known for coffee, North Star pleasantly surprises. This is a converted house with spacious front-and-back decks for warm/dry weather sippin' and MAX train watchin'. And if the music don't suit ya, that's why they make headphones. Now hopefully the white belts don't discover this one. (Oh my gawd, Zinester's Guide, white belts are soooo...2003!) (sg)

Late Night Eats

Javier's Taco Shop #2   *121 N Lombard St. / 503-286-3186 / Open 24 hours, 7 days a week* Javier's has become a mixed bag. At one point, the burritos were always good, now it's not so. Sometimes they hit it, often they don't. And it's a bit out there (location wise). But it is open 24-7, which right now is the ONLY thing Javier's has going for it. So be warned.

Other Mercantile-type Operations

Blue Moon Camera & Machine   *8417 N Lombard St / (503) 978-0333 / Mo-Fr 9a-6p, Sa 9a-5p* A treasure & museum of sorts. Not your ordinary camera shop. Don't expect one-hour service or support for your digital photography needs. Blue Moon specializes in durable machines & quality processing. They sell what they shoot & print as if it were for them. A great resource for out of production film formats. Even if you're not into photography, go behold the typewriters. An impressive collection of refurbished manual writing appliances awaits you. Be nice to the staff and they may let you pet them. (ms)

Parks

Cathedral park   *N. Edison & Pittsburgh* A park right directly underneath the eastside of the St. Johns Bridge. The name of the park and surrounding neighborhood is derived from the gothic towers of the bridge, reminiscent of an old cathedral. It's a great place to catch views of the bridge, the west hills, and the river's traffic. And it's thought to be haunted! As the legend goes: "Thelma Taylor, a happy 15 year old high school student, was abducted in 1949. Her abductor took her to this area (which back then was undeveloped brush area). She was bound, raped and held for almost a week before she finally died. There's reports every summer of screams coming from the park, but there is nothing there. The screams can be heard to this day...screams of a girl caught and bound, with no hope of escape." Spooky! (This info was culled from the site "The Ghosts of North Portland" at http://home.attbi.com/~hmb01/ghosts/ghosts.htm.) They also filmed a scene from My Own Private Idaho here. Access via N Baltimore Ave, west of downtown St. Johns. (sg)

Columbia Park   *N. Lombard & Woolsey* Historically, this was the first park to be created by the short-lived City of Albina, which is now part of Portland. Picnic areas, ball courts, and tons and tons of Douglas Firs. Also includes a pool. Located between N Winchell, N Chautauqua, N Willamette Blvd, and N Woolsey (sg)

Smith and Bybee Lakes Park Lying on the floodplain of the Columbia, Smith and Bybee lakes is a freshwater estuary, at the convergence of the Columbia River and Columbia Slough. The marshy area is good for observing a variety of wildlife, or just to chill out and get away from the heaviness of urban living for a bit.   If it wasn't for the constant drone of I-5 traffic (a couple miles off, even) and the occasional train noise, you would think you were far from the city, when in reality, it's only about 8 miles from downtown. A paved path leads from the entry point to a couple enclosed bird-watching shelters. The entrance is off N Marine Drive west of N Portland Road (a couple miles east of Kelley Point Park). (sg)

Restaurants

Tulip Bakery   *8322 N Lombard St / (503) 286-3444 / Tu-Fr 6a-5p, Sa 8a-5p, Su 9a-1p* Owned and operated by the same family for over 50 years, the Tulip is a classic old fashion bakery. Go early for fresh bread & donuts, late afternoon for cookies hot out of the oven. Respectable selection of cheap & tasty day olds. Totally worth the trip from any other point in the city! (ms)

Tulip Baker (sg)

Outer Northeast
Donuts

Annie's Donuts *3449 NE 72nd Av (at Sandy/Fremont) / 503-284-2752* The quest for a good donut is a tough one in this town. If you're from one of those places "back east" and are used to a Dunkin Donuts, Krispy Kreme, or (insert your local donut chain here) on practically every block, Portland must seem like a veritable donut desert. When a decent donut shop is found, it is like water to the thirsty man. Factors that would ordinarily be considered obstacles, like distance, are quickly forgotten. Annie's is one of those decent donut shops, and despite being at least a couple miles from the closest "hip" district, devotees travel the distance to sample the savory treats, like pilgrims to Mecca. Annie's is the ying to Voodoo's yang in Portland's Donutverse. Voodoo is only open at night, Annie's open during the day. Voodoo is hip and quirky, Annie's unpretentious and plain. Voodoo has punks and hipsters hanging out, Annie's seems to be solely occupied by old men reading the newspaper (and if that doesn't speak old-school donut shop, I don't know what does!) I'm not saying one is better than the other, but if you solely sing the praises of Voodoo, I suggest heading out to Roseway to see what you're missing. (Sorry, no vegan donuts.) (sg)

(sg)

Ever-nebulous "Other" Category

Dignity Village *9325 NE Sunderland Ave. (off of NE 33rd Ave near NE Marine Drive)* In December 2000, a group of homeless individuals decided to do something to get themselves out of the doorways. They set up five tents on public land, and Dignity Village was born. Through hard work, determination, public support, and resourcefulness,

Dignity Village has grown and thrived to be a self-governing village that houses formerly homeless people with the city's approval. The residents build their own shelters and take part in the village decisions. Dignity is currently in the process of moving on to a new phase by establishing a perma-site based on their on-going model. In its current location, Dignity Village makes use of environmentally-friendly materials such as strawbale housing, and uses wind-generated electricity. Dignity Village serves as a unique model of one solution for homelessness, and is one of the oldest on-going homeless villages in the country. It has gained interest from homeless advocates from around the world. Visitors are welcome to drop by. (jv)

Other Mercantile-type Operations

The Grotto   *NE 85th Ave. and Sandy Blvd. / 503-254-7371*   The Grotto, or as it's officially known, "National Sanctuary of Our Sorrowful Mother", is a 62-acre Catholic Shrine and botanical garden located on the fringe of the inner city (near the airport). The history of the Grotto goes way back to 1923, when one Friar Ambrose Mayer purchased the property from the Union Pacific Railroad, with the intent of starting his dream project. What you'll find here is lots of trees, gardens, shrines, Catholic type-stuff (they even have mass here), and The Gift Shop. People who have ventured to the Grotto either find it creepy, fascinating, or fascinatingly creepy. South of the Grotto you'll find Rocky Butte (see Parks listing), and hidden away to the east at NE Skidmore St and NE 92nd, you'll find some well maintained BMX-bike tracks tucked into the woods.

It's My Pleasure   *3106 NE 64th at (NE corner of) Sandy Blvd. / 503-280-8080*   A small, women-run sex shop. Yoni-fied, with lots of rainbow flag merchandise, erotic massage oils and lotions (don't test out the lotion, it will keep lubricating as you try to rub it into your skin, causing you to smell like an erotic masseuse forever-more). They also have an excellent selection of dildos and vibrators, with handmade harnesses made from denim and recycled bike tubes! Great. They give you Hershey's Kisses with each purchase, which comes in a discreet purple bag. Enjoy! (ng)

Restaurants

Café Be Van   *6846 NE Sandy Blvd / 503-287-1418 / find new hours*   This Vietnamese bistro tags itself the "deli" of the new generation. I believe this means this isn't your father's Vietnamese joint, eh? Be Van serves up great Vietnamese sandwiches a-plenty, most under three dollars. Their veggie sandwich ($2.50) comes with tasty strips of tofu on fresh French bread. Just make sure to say "no mayo" if you don't want it! Other features are bubble tea,and a Vietnamese Waffle ($1.75) made with coconut milk. Be Van offers free internet, so you can look at Homestar Runner while waiting for your order. (sg)

Fairley's Pharmacy   *7206 NE Sandy Blvd (at Fremont) / 503- 284-1159*   The old-school independent drugstore, the type that contains a soda fountain, is a very endangered species in not only Portland, but the world. Many Portlandites fondly fetishised the pharmacy at NE 60th and Belmont (open transom, anyone?), but it recently closed. Fairley's is one of the very few soda-fountain pharmacies left here, so if you want to get a Cherry Phosphate, make sure you head here. How long will it last? I don't know, but now Fairley's has Wi-Fi (???) and an espresso machine, so you can work on your laptop while sippin' a root beer float or latté. (sg)

New Cali Sandwiches   *6620 NE Glisan St / 503-254-9842 / Mo-Fr 10a-7pm, Sa 10a-6p* Cheap and tasty Vietnamese sandwiches. Full array of meats, if you please. Vegetarian sandwich with tofu only $2.50! Just make sure you say "no mayo" if you don't want it! (sg)

Theaters

Roseway Theatre   *7229 NE Sandy Blvd / 503-287-8119 / regular fare $6, showings before 6pm and all day Monday $5* Built in 1924 and opened in 1925, the single screen Roseway has been in continuous operation for 79 years. Passing through many hands over the years, the Roseway almost closed for good in the 90's. In 1999, the Kane siblings bought the Roseway, determined to return it to its original luster. The Roseway, like the Moreland, is one of the few independent theaters in the city that still shows first-run Hollywood fare. Its well preserved Art Deco interior and exterior makes the Roseway a landmark in this district. (sg)

Thrift Stores

Better Bargains   *10209 NE Sandy Blvd / M-F 9-8:30, Sat 9-7, Sun 10-6* This one's a little far out there, but it's worth a look. Substantial discounts will make it worth your while: Wednesdays and Saturdays everything is 30% off, and Monday is senior citizens' day, so bring the grandfolks. If you donate a bag of stuff, you get a coupon for 40% off a bag of their goods! (en)

Roseway Theatre (sg)

Outer Southeast

Bars

The Lutz *4639 SE Woodstock Blvd. / 503-774-0353* Pabst. Pabst. Pabst. Supposedly this SE watering hole is where the current Pabst craze has started (at least that's according to the New York Times!) And video poker. The Lutz also serves as the waiting room for The Delta Café (they'll call you when your table's ready). Don't miss it.

(sm)

Coffeehouses, Teahouses and the like

Bipartisan Café *7901 SE Stark St / (503) 253-1051* Are we really serious? A good coffee place only (gasp!) THREE BLOCKS FROM 82ND? THE AXIS OF ALL EVIL IN THE PORTLAND AREA? I mean, from outside Bipartisan you can...actually...see 82nd Avenue! Yes my friends, this is no typo. Located in the commerical heart of the Montavilla neighborhood, a land of little in the way of culinary pleasures, save Flying Pie, Ya Hala, and now this. Bipartisan is a good Portland coffeeshop that meets all the qualifications. Stumptown Coffee, good homemade pies, hardwood floors, big windows, an airy interior, and great staff. The presidential decorations (depicting most every president since there were presidents) may irk those "staunch radical anarchists" (who pro'lly won't leave inner N/NE anyway), but where else can you find an actual circa 2000 Palm Beach County (Fla.) voting machine, with the infamous butterfly ballot? Well, where can you, wise guy? (sg)

The Ugly Mug *8017 SE 13th Ave / (503) 230-2010 / 6:30am-10pm Mo-Fr, 7am-10pm Sa-Su* About every couple weeks I like to take a "field trip" to Sellwood, a neighborhood still in SE Portland yet detached enough that it feels like another town. The cruise alongside the Willamette is beautiful, the views of the city from Sellwood Blvd, but the coffee? Well...nothing really impressed me down there, whether it be quality of coffee or atmosphere of shop. Luckily the Ugly Mug came along. This joint has got the Stumptown, it's got the atmosphere, it's got the mug-shaped bike rack in front, and now it's got the beer (that's why it's open til 10!) I can get so amped up here it can almost make a trip to the Bins bearable. Almost! (sg)

Parks

Beggars-Tick Wildlife Refuge *SE 111th at Springwater Corridor Trail* This small park features a wide variety of habitats including open water, shrub/scrub marsh, cattail/smartweed marsh, and forested wetland. The refuge also serves as a wintering spot for waterfowl. Alternate entrance at SE 111th just north of SE Foster. (sg)

Leach Botanical Gardens *6704 SE 122 Ave. / 503-823-9503* Practically unknown by most of the folks I know, this plant park is hidden in a wooden hollow along Johnson Creek south of Foster Road. The nine-acre garden features a collection of over 2,000 species of plants, many of which are Northwest native plants. Also featured is a composting demonstration site. To get there from the Springwater Trail, go south along SE 122nd, crossing Powell. Be careful, it's a windy road! (sg)

Oaks Amusement Park (cm)

Oaks Amusement Park *At the end of SE Oaks Park Way, off SE Spokane St (by the Sellwood Bridge). / 503-236-5722 (rink)* Once known as the "Coney Island of the Northwest", originally opened May 30, 1905, making it one of the oldest amusement parks in the country, and the only amusement park in Portland. In keeping with the design of other "Trolley Parks" across the country, most of its visitors "back in the day" disembarked from trolley cars which from downtown Portland to Oregon City. The trolleys are gone, but the tracks are still there, the park sandwiched between them and the Willamette River. And the rides are still there, so if you're in the mood for good ol' carney style fun in the summer, head here. Don't forget the Roller Rink, which is open year-round! The rides only operate spring to early fall (daily in summer, weekends-only any other time). You can also access the park via the new OMSI-Springwater bicycle path.

Oaks Bottom Wildlife Refuge This green area, wedged between the Willamette River and the Sellwood neighborhood, is an undeveloped park where you can see what the banks of the river looked like before the city was born. An unpaved trail runs the length of the park, starting at the SE Milwaukie entrance, heading south along the eastbank of a pond (good for bird-watching) and ends at the entrances of Oaks Park and Sellwood Park. Good place for dog-walkin. New-ish is the OMSI-Springwater trail, which is a paved bicycle and walking trail that parallels the old Portland Traction rail line. This path starts at SE 4th Ave. south of SE Division Place by the Ross Island Bridge (watch out for all the Ross Island cement trucks!) and runs all the way south to the Sellwood Bridge at SE Spokane St. There is a connecting trail to SE Milwaukie mid-way along the trail as well. If you need a quick connection from Sellwood to downtown via bike, this is it! Make sure you check out the gi-normous blue heron mural on the wall of the mausoleum (look across the pond from the trail). (sg)

Sellwood Neighborhood (jm)

Reed College Canyon *access from Botsford Drive off SE 28th (just north of Woodstock)* Despite what you may think of Reed College and its students (Reedies), the campus is a pretty nice place to go. The jewel of it is the Reed Canyon, a 26 acre natural area running lengthwise west-east through the heart of the property. The brook here is Crystal Springs, its source near SE 37th in the east and then flowing westward to Johnson Creek. Crystal Springs Creek is the last free-flowing stream in this part of town, and its lake is "the only naturally occurring pond (or lake) remaining in the inner-city area." There is a nature trail that circles the ravine and is a great respite from the urban-ness that surrounds it. The lush canopy of trees above the steep sides of the ravine provide great relief on a hot summer day. If you don't want to enter from the main entrance, there are a couple of sneak entrances, at the deadend of SE 37th Ave a couple blocks south of Steele, and at the deadend of SE Reedway just to the west of 39th. (sg)

Sellwood Park. *Enter at SE 7th Ave, two blocks north of Tacoma St.* Sellwood is your typical Portland park, complete with ball fields, picnic areas, restrooms, and Douglas Firs. It adjoins Oaks Bottom wildlife refuge, Oaks Park, and Sellwood Riverfront Park. (sg)

Sellwood Riverfront Park *Enter at SE Spokane/SE 6th at foot of Sellwood Bridge.* This park is on the banks of the Willamette in far SE Portland, Good place to picnic and watch the boats on the River (there's a boat launch here as well.) Also a good view of the Sellwood Bridge and the ghastly condominiums that border it. You can now connect to the OMSI-Springwater Trail here (see Oaks Bottom listing) (sg)

Tideman Johnson Park Named after a pioneer family, this li'l park is nestled in a gorge along the Johnson Creek. Mostly in its natural state, this wooded secluded area is a nice hideaway when the city gets too much on ya. Also good for observing Johnson Creek, one of the last free-flowing brooks in the city. Alternate entrance is at SE 39th and SE Tenino.

(sg)

Pizza

Flying Pie Pizzeria *7804 SE Stark St / (503) 254-2016 / 11a-10p Su-Th, 11a-11p Fr-Sa* While East Coast Style pizza is definitely my thing, every once in a while I'll make a trip out to the far side of Tabor for Flying Pie. Located in Montavilla's "downtown", Flying Pie feels worn in, but in the good old-school pizza parlor type of way. Yes, pizza parlor, the type of place that coach would take the little league after a game on Saturday. Red vinyl benches and sports memorabilia on the walls. Pizza parlor! If you show up between 11-3 on weekdays you can order a huge-arsed slice topped your way. If you are of the vegan persuasion, that means you can order it sans frommage, or if you dare, get soy cheese on it! And don't forget the bread sticks. (sg)

Theaters

Moreland Theatre *6712 SE Milwaukie Ave (near Bybee Blvd) / 503-236-5257* Opened in 1926, the Moreland has been in continuous operation. The Moreland has always kept the same name through its 80 year history. Also, the Moreland is unique because it still has a single screen and still shows first-run Hollywood cinema fare (versus second-run or arthouse fare that many of the historic theaters in town). The interior and exterior have been preserved, retaining the look and feel of a Deco era cinema. (sg)

Thrift Stores

The Bins (a.k.a Goodwill Outlet) *1740 SE Ochoco St (near McLaughlin) / 503-230-2076 / Mo-Fr 9a-9p, Sa 9a-7p, Su 10a-6p* You have to be in a special mood to go to the bins. Are you ready to get your hands dirty enough that touching your face could lead to certain death? Ready to punch your way out if you've got an exceptional find? Then you're prepared for this amazing thrifting adventure. At the bins you can buy clothes for 1.50 per POUND, and other housewares and books for less than that. It takes a lot of digging (as there are actual 100 foot long bins of unsorted merchandise for you to look through), but at times you could find amazing things for insanely cheap prices. Watch out for the daring old women who race to the newest merchandise and will gladly knock you on the ground and step on your face if it can get them closer to that vintage mohair sweater! (ng)

Delta Café (ik)

Bridges

The Broadway Bridge was designed by Ralph Modjeski and completed in 1913. This unique drawbridge stands over a quarter-mile long at 1,736 feet.

Broadway Bridge *Broadway between NW and N, connects NW Lovejoy and N Interstate* The Broadway is a drawbridge completed in 1913. It is a double-leaf Rall type Bascule drawbridge, unique in Portland and very rare otherwise. (A bascule drawbridge is "seesaw" style, the two "draws" lift up away from each other to accomodate for riverine traffic) The Rall system uses complicated rolling lift mechanisms, meaning long delays when the bridge goes up (usually 10-20 minutes).

USAGE: Automotive traffic, pedestrians, bicycles

OWNER: Multnomah County

BICYCLE INFO: Bicycles have bike lanes up until the bridge itself, and then are directed onto the sidewalks. The Broadway is the most popular connection for bicyclists from N/NE to downtown and the westside.

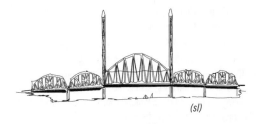

(sl)

TECHNICAL INFO: Total length 1,613 ft (492m), main span 278 feet long (85m), clearance from river 70 ft (21m). Painted "Golden Gate" Red (aka International Orange) (sg)

Burlington Northern Railroad Bridge 5.1 (aka St Johns Railroad Bridge) *on the Willamette River about one mile south of the St Johns Bridge* This bridge was built in 1908 to complete the then Northern Pacific (now part of Burlington Northern Santa Fe) mainline north to Seattle. At the time it was a swing bridge, meaning that the center span would "swing" open to allow for boat traffic. Even though it was the longest swing span in the world, modern maritime needs led to the spans' obsolescence, and in 1989 the bridge was retrofitted with a vertical lift span. The twin towers can be seen for miles around.

USAGE: Freight trains (BNSF, UP), Amtrak

OWNERSHIP: Burlington Northern Santa Fe Railway

Burnside Bridge

(cl)

BICYCLE INFO: No bikes!

TECHNICAL INFO: 516 ft (157m) long lift span, vertical clearance 200 ft (61m), fourth highest lift bridge in the world. (sg)

Burnside Bridge *Burnside St* The Burnside is a bascule type drawbridge that opened in 1926. Architecturally speaking, the most significant thing about the bridge are the twin towers at each end of the movable section, done up in Italian Renaissance style. Culturally speaking, the significant things about the bridge is what goes on UNDERNEATH it. Under the westside is Portland's famed tourist trap Saturday Market, and under the eastside is the world-renowned Burnside Skatepark.

USERS: Automotive traffic, pedestrians, bicycles

OWNER: Multnomah County

BICYCLE INFO: Bike lanes run in both directions on the bridge itself, though the connections on both ends are a bit spotty, forcing you to suddenly merge with

Fremont Bridge

(dm)

fast-moving traffic.

TECHNICAL INFO: Total length 2,308 ft (703 m), center span 252 ft (77 m), lowered bridge 64 feet (20 m) above water (sg)

Fremont Bridge *I-405, between Pearl/Northwest and Albina* Opened in 1973, the Fremont is the youngest of Portland's Willamette River crossings. It's beautiful design is due to the Marquam (I-5) Bridge's ugliness--the Portland Art Commission was brought in to aid with design so there wouldn't be such an uproar. (We Portlanders are very particular about our bridges!) Its gentle arch (once the longest tied-arch bridge in the world) dominates the skyline. And peregrine falcons nest on the underside of the span, look closely and you may see one soaring around the bridge!

USAGE: Automotive traffic

OWNER: State of Oregon

(dw)

BICYCLES: Prohibited

TECHNICAL INFO: 2,152 ft (656m) long, main span 1,255 ft (383m) long, top of arch 381 ft (116m) above the river, clearance above river 175 ft (53m) (sg)

Hawthorne Bridge *connects SW Main/Madison on the west, SE Madison/Hawthorne* *on the east* Aah, the Hawthorne! This bridge is possibly Portlanders most-favorite bridge, and it's at least the city's most distinctive bridge. Many postcards feature the photogenic structure, and it can even draw big-time Hollywood directors to shoot crappy big-budget movies here (see The Hunted). Anyways...The Hawthorne Bridge is a truss bridge with a vertical lift span, and is the oldest vertical lift bridge in operation in the United States! Built in 1910, it's the city's oldest bridge but still does a lot of work. A major rehabilitation effort was undertaken in 1998-9, giving us the 10 foot wide sidewalks and green-and-red color scheme. The low clearance over the river means the drawbridge opens frequently, so it's common to be stuck waiting for the bridge.

USERS: Automotive traffic, pedestrians, bicycles.

OWNER: Multnomah County

BICYCLE INFO: The Hawthorne is the city's busiest bicycle bridge, with 1,500 bicycle crossings daily. The westside connects convieniently with Waterfront Park and the downtown grid, and the eastside connects to the Eastbank Esplanade and the Madison/Hawthorne bikelanes. Bicyclists must use the sidewalk (it's not fun riding on a steel grid deck)

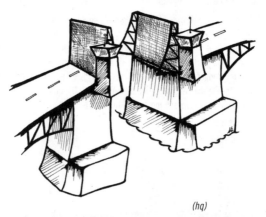

(hq)

TECHNICAL INFO: Total length 1,382 ft (421m), consisting of five fixed spans and one 244 ft. long (74m) vertical lift span, clearance 49 ft (15m) above water (sg)

Morrison Bridge *between SW Washington/Alder on the west, SE Morrison/Belmont on the east* Its current version opened in 1958, the Morrison is a busy workhorse bridge spanning downtown with the Central Eastside. It's yet another Portland drawbridge, a "Chicago Style" bascule bridge (see drawing for how it opens). Built during the "we need to build a lot of stuff fast" period of bridge engineering, the Morrison is not much to look at. The "air traffic control tower" styled bridge towers (with slanted windows) are the bridge's most distinctive feature. The bridge is one of the largest mechanical structures in Oregon, due to its 940 ton (!) counterweights with 36 ft. tall gears located inside each of the piers.

USERS: Automotive traffic, pedestrians, bicycles.

OWNER: Multnomah County

BICYCLE INFO: While its central location would be great for a bicycle crossing, it really sucks to have to use a bicycle this bridge. For one, bicycles are prohibited from the roadway and must stay on the sidewalk. And using the sidewalk means using three separate series of stairs (up and down) to go around all the highway on-ramps. This sucks for pedestrians also Sometime in the near future the Morrison will become more bicycle and pedestrian friendly, until then, use one of the other bridges instead.

TECHNICAL INFO: Total length of bridge 760 ft (232m), draw span 284 ft (87m) (sg)

Marquam Bridge   *connects I-5 on both sides of the river* Opened in 1966, the Marquam opened Portland to through driving on I-5 between BC to Mexico. The double deckered cantilever bridge sits high above the river, dominating the scenery around. The bridge itself is boring, a victim of the Vanilla School of Engineering that built the nation's Interstate Highway System, where economy of design and cost trumped aestectics. It infuriated many Portlanders at the time of completion, and led to the Portland Art Commission helping with the design of the next freeway bridge (Fremont-1973). Great views of the city and Mt Hood abound from the bridge, for the half-a-minute commuter traffic zips across it at least. If you're a pedestrian or bicyclist, you're out of luck (at least until BridgePedal).

USERS: Automotive traffic ONLY

OWNER: State of Oregon

BICYCLES PROHIBITED.

TECHNICAL INFO: Length of main span 440 ft (134m), length of two side spans 301 ft (92m) each, vertical clearance of the lower deck is 130 ft (40m) above the river, upper deck 15 ft (5m) above the lower (sg)

Ross Island Bridge   *connects ramp nonsense on the west side, Powell Blvd (US 26) on the east* Opened in 1926, the Ross Island is named after the sandy isle in the Willamette directly to the south of the bridge. Its cantilever truss span is a subtle beauty (much like Portland itself), the more you look at it, the more you appreciate it. The Ross Island was the city's busiest bridge from its time of completion up to the opening of the Marquam Bridge.

USERS: Automotive traffic, pedestrians, bicycles.

OWNER: State of Oregon

BICYCLE INFO: The Ross Island offers remedial bicycle facilities. Bicyclists must use a narrow sidewalk and then negotiate their way around a series of off-ramps on the westside, pretty dangerous. ODOT rehabilitated the bridge a few years back, but improved the bicycle access very little, which seems to happen with all their recent bridge projects (see St Johns)

St. John's

TECHNICAL INFO: Longest span 535 ft
(163m) (sg)

Sellwood Bridge *connects SW Marquam/*
Riverside on the west, SE Tacoma on the east
The Sellwood, along with the St Johns, are the
least-seen Willamette River Bridges to the casual
visitor, mostly due to their distance. The Sellwood
Bridge is about 5 miles south of downtown, and is more
useful for connecting the far-reaches of the metro area
than for the city itself. The two-lane truss bridge opened in
1925, at the time the county must have thought that many
lanes would suffice. Unfortunately for modern use it does not,
and the bridge is overused beyond its capacity. The capacity of
32 tons was lowered to 10 in 2004 after bridge inspectors found
numerous cracks in the span. Now busses and trucks can't use
the bridge and the question posed is: will the Sellwood be repaired
or rebuilt? Enjoy the current bridge and the great views from it while
you can, because it's not going to last.

Fremont
Broadway
Steel
Burnside
Morrison
Hawthorne
Marquam
Ross Island

USERS: Automotive traffic, pedestrians, bicycles

OWNER: Multnomah County

BICYCLE INFO: The Sellwood is a crucial link in the Willamette River
loop, but on-bridge facilities suck. You are required to walk your
bike across on the very narrow sidewalk.

TECHNICAL INFO: Total length 1,971 ft (601m) with four
continuous spans, two center span length 300 ft (92m) each,
two outside span length 246 ft (75m), clearance 75 ft (23m)

Sellwood

(km)

(nb)

above river (sg)

St Johns Bridge *US 30 Bypass between St Johns and Linnton* The St Johns bridge is Portland's only suspension bridge, and not often seen by the casual visitor (it is about six miles from downtown). Opened in 1931, at the time it was the longest suspension bridge west of Detroit (other bridges have surpassed its size since then, most notably the Golden Gate Bridge). Painted green, the bridge tends to blend in against the West Hills. It's a quite beautiful bridge and a symbol of pride for the St Johns neighborhood. The gothic arched towers and eastside support beams lended the name Cathedral Park to the greenspace and neighborhood below.

USAGE: Automotive traffic, pedestrians, bicycles

OWNER: State of Oregon

BICYCLE INFO: The St. Johns is a highly un-bikeable bridge. Bicycles must use a narrow sidewalk (after construction is done), the westside approach is steep and bicyclists must ride on a busy street. Since the bridge is a high one, going over it means making a big climb in elevation from the east. There was hope that during the current bridge work the bicycle situation would be improved, but the pleas from bicycle advocates fell on deaf ears at ODOT. Thankfully, the St Johns Bridge doesn't fulfil a vital bicycle link for in-town transit, but does come in useful for accessing Sauvie Island from the eastside.

TECHNICAL INFO: Two Gothic towers 408 ft tall (124 m), 1207 ft (368 m) center span 205 feet (62 m) above the Willamette River. Total length 2,067

(eb)

feet (630 m) (sg)

Steel Bridge   *connects NW Everett/Glisan/Front on the west, N Interstate/ Oregon/Multnomah on the east* The Steel Bridge is a very special bridge. It is the only double-deck vertical lift bridge with independent lift decks (the lower deck can retract into the upper deck without the upper deck moving) in THE WORLD, and the second-oldest vertical lift bridge in North America (the first being our own Hawthorne Bridge)! The Steel was built in 1912 by the Union Pacific Railroad and its primary function was as a railroad bridge, but it accomodates much more than that! It's the most diverse bridge maybe anywhere (as you'll see by the users below). Its functionality was increased with the opening of the pedestrian walkway on the lower deck in 2001, completing the downtown waterfront loop. It's quite the experience to ride your bike along the bottom deck while a freight train goes rumbling by!

USERS: upper deck: automotive traffic, MAX light rail, pedestrians, bicycles

lower deck: freight trains (UP, BNSF), Amtrak, pedestrians, bicycles

OWNER: Union Pacific Railroad, upper deck leased to Oregon Dept. of Transportation and subleased to TriMet

BICYCLES: the top deck is remedially bikeable, though narrow sidewalks and steep approaches from the west doesn't make it that fun. Most bicycles use the bottom deck to get between downtown and Waterfront Park to the Eastbank Esplanade.

TECHNICAL INFO: through truss double lift bridge, main span 211 ft (64 m) long, lower deck 26 ft (8 m) above water, upper deck 72 ft (22 m) above water, 163 ft (50 m) of total vertical clearance when both decks are fully raised (sg)

The Multnomah County Library System

Multnomah County Library (Central Library) *801 SW 10th Av / 503.988.5123 / 10a-6p Mo, 10a-8p Tu-We, 10a-6p Th-Sa, 12-5p Su* Portland has a great library system (which is run by the county, by the way.) The "granddaddy" of the libraries is Central Library downtown, located 801 SW 10th Ave. (503.988.5123) First opened in September 1913, and extensively renovated in 1996-97, Central Library houses over 875 tons of books (!)and other library materials. Central has three floors; checkout, Fiction, and the Beverly Cleary Children's Room (she's from here, y'know!) on the ground; Periodicals, Science, Business, Rare Books, and Government Documents on the second; Art, Music, and Humanities on the third. Central has 130 computer search stations, some with Internet that you can use for one hour (and despite the vast number of computers, they are ALWAYS BUSY!)

Multnomah County Central Library Picture File (at Central Library) On the 3rd Floor in the Henry Falling Art and Music Library. The picture file is an invaluable resource to the zinester. What is it, you ask? Well, have you ever thought, "damn, I could use a lot of pictures of people dancing..." That's what the picture file is for! Just go up to the information desk in the Art and Music Library on the 3rd floor and say "hi! I am looking for pictures of [insert topic here]." The librarian will look to see if they have a file on that subject, and if so, they give you a card to take to the picture file desk. There a different librarian will give you the file, which you can't take out the library, but there are 10-cent photocopies just around the corner. I wrote a zine that I filled with dozens of pictures of robots from the picture file. Save yourself the time of looking through hundreds of old magazines for just the right pics- the picture file has already done that for you. It's a zinester's dream.

Hillsdale Branch *1525 SW Sunset Blvd / 503.988.5388 / 10a-8p Mo-Tu, 10a-6p We-Sa, 12-5 Su*

Hollywood Branch *4040 NE Tillamook St / 503.988.5391 / 10a-8p Mo-Tu, 10a-6p We-Sa, 12-5 Su* This one's got a map of Beverly Cleary/Ramona the Brave landmarks in it!

Albina Branch *3605 NE 15th Av inside Nature's Place Branch / 503.988.5362 / 10a-6p Mo, 12-8p Tu-We, 10a-6p Th-Sa, 12-5p Su*

Belmont Branch *1038 SE 39th Av / 503.988.5382 / 10a-6p Mo, 12-8p Tu-We, 10a-6p Th-Sa, 12-5p Su*

Gregory Heights Branch *7921 NE Sandy Blvd / 503.988.5386 / 10a-6p Mo, 12-8p Tu-We, 10a-6p Th-Sa, 12-5p Su*

North Portland Branch *512 N Killingsworth St at Commercial Av Branch / 503.988.5394 / 10a-6p Mo, 12-8p Tu-We, 10a-6p Th-Sa, 12-5p Su* This branch may be haunted!

Northwest Branch *2300 NW Thurman St / 503.988.5560 / 10a-6p Mo, 12-8p Tu-We, 10a-6p Th-Sa, 12-5p Su*

Sellwood-Moreland Branch *7860 SE 13th Av / 503.988.5398 / 10a-6p Mo, 12-8p Tu-We, 10a-6p Th-Sa, 12-5p Su*

Woodstock Branch *6008 SE49th Av at Woodstock Blvd Branch / 503.988.5399 / 10a-6p Mo, 12-8p Tu-We, 10a-6p Th-Sa, 12-5p Su*

Bicycling in Portland

Without a doubt, Portland is a great place to bicycle in. Bike lanes are abundant, the city government actually cares about the plight of cyclists, and motorists tend to be more aware and less antagonistic than in other places. Obviously things are far from perfect, but can you realistically find biketopia anywhere?

Probably the best gauge of an area's bikeability is by counting the number of people you see bicycling. And Stumptown's streets are filled with them! Whether it be the spandex-clad "top-o-the-line" scorcher preparing for her next race, or the bike messenger type with a tiny U-Lock in back pocket riding a single-speed, or crazed clowns riding fluorescent-colored choppers, or just an ordinary-dressin' person on a 3-speed, baskets laden with groceries, you'll find every type of bicycle and bicycle rider here.

Portland was made to be bicycled. Most places within the central city can be easily reached within a half-hour bike ride. Streets here generally have low-to-moderate traffic amounts, and six-lane-plus mega-boulevards found in many western cities are few, mostly found in the suburban hinterlands. While not "flat as a pancake" like the Windy City, major hills are rare (the notable exceptions being the West Hills, the short-yet-steep Alameda Ridge, the bluffs lining the river in North Portland, and the buttes that pepper the East Portland landscape) so the constant up-and-downs prevalent in Seattle and San Francisco can pretty much be avoided here. And our winters are mild, so riding year-round is possible. Of course, you'll have to deal with the rains, but get the approps rain gear and you'll cope.

Riding a bicycle is, in my humble opinion, the best way to explore this city. While Tri-Met is reliable and extensive, it doesn't offer the same flexibility you get with a bike. Walking is great and PDX is a pedestrian-friendly city, but the bicycle gives you extended range. And a bike can get to places that a car never will, like trails and secret wooded spots.

(na)

Having a bike allows you to explore every durn neighborhood in this burg, and you'll have the urge to seek out more. So find yourself a bike, whether it be cruiser, 3-speed, BMX, road bike, mountain bike, etc, and hit the streets of the Rose City! (sg)

Bicycle Shops

Bicycle Repair Collective
4438 SE Belmont St / 503-233-0564 / Mo-Sa 10-6 Portland's original community-oriented bicycle shop (founded in 1976 at what is now the main Citybikes) that offers space to work on your own cycle. They also offer bicycle repair classes, and will work on your bicycle for a nominal fee. (sg)

(sl)

Bike Gallery
1001 SW Salmon St / 503-222-3821 High-end bicycle shop. Repair services and classes offered. (sg)

Bike Gallery (Northeast)
5329 NE Sandy Blvd / 503-281-9800

City Bikes
1914 SE Ankeny St / 503-239-0553 / Mo-Fr 11-7, Sa-Su 11-5 This worker-owned cooperative has two convenient locations on Ankeny. The main shop (1914 SE Ankeny St) specializes in bike repair and used parts, and the Annex (734 SE Ankeny St) specializes in used bike sales (which they overhaul on-premises), bicycle accessories, and bike rentals. Staff is helpful and knowledgeable. Make sure you schedule an appointment early for bicycle work, since they tend to get quite backed up, especially in summer. Bike rentals available. (sg)

CityBikes kiosk and Virgen de Guadalupe shrine
SE 8th at SE Ankeny St Outside of Citybikes is a new cob kiosk and bench, a shrine to the Virgin Guadalupe, and a new community garden where part of a parking lot has been depaved.

City Bikes Annex
734 SE Ankeny St / 503-239-6951 / Mo-Fr 11-7, Sa-Su 11-5 Look for the mural and art on the side of the building!

Community Cycling Center
1700 NE Alberta St / 503-288-8864 / Tu-Fr 12-7, Sa 10-6, Su 12-5 Friendly and cheap place to buy used/new bike parts. Bikestand, tools, and advice available for free, as well as inexpensive fixes by the volunteers and workers. Many opportunities to volunteer here are also available. Community oriented, non-profit shop. Offers bicycle repair classes. (sg)

Coventry Cycle Works   *2025 SE Hawthorne Blvd / 503-230-7723 / Tu-Sa 10-6, Su 1-5* Cozy neighborhood shop that specializes in recumbent sales. (sg)

Missing Link Bicycle Shop   *5709 NE Fremont St / 503-740-3539 / Mo-Fr 11a-7p, Sa-Su 11a-5p* This neighborhood bicycle shop once operated out of a van that would make housecalls. Now firmly planted on the outer edge of Rose City Park (where it meets "The Cully"), Missing Link offers a full line of services and accessories, and also sells used bikes. If you're jonesin' to make your bike a "fixie", Missing Link can do that for you as well! (sg)

North Portland Bike Works   *3951 N Mississippi Av / 503-287-1098 / Mo-Sa 11-6* A non-profit bicycle shop specializing in affordable used and consignment bicycles, new supplies, and service for the neighborhood. Many programs available, and many opportunities to volunteer and earn credit. Repair classes offered. Community night occurs once a month where space can be used for free. Women's only night (trans-friendly) is every Wednesday. (sg)

PSU Bicycle Cooperative   *SW Corner of SW 5th and Harrison St (inside parking garage) / 503-725-9006 / Mo- Fr 10a-3p when PSU is in session, otherwise call for appt.* The PSU Bicycle Cooperative is a super tiny, super cool campus bikeshop servicing the PSU community. Students, faculty, staff, and alumni are all invited to become members. Currently, the annual membership fee is just $10. Members are allowed to use the space and tools during regular hours, get bicycle repair assistance and training from Coop staff, purchase parts and merchandise at a special discounted rate, enroll in Coop-sponsored workshops, and utilize our covered and gated bike parking facility during daytime hours. Not a member of the PSU Community? The Coop still wants to help. If you have an emergency or just need to borrow the nearest bike pump, please don't hesitiate to stop by there. (is)

River City Bicycles   *706 SE Martin Luther King Jr Blvd / 503-233-5973 / Mo-Fr 10-7, Sa 10-5, Su 12-5 (stays open 1 hr later each night in summer)* Mid-to-high-end shop with loads and loads of bikes and accessories. Full repair shops. Offers bicycle repair and "how to commute" classes. Theyll also make you a free espresso-based drink while you wait for your bike repair! Look for the bike sculptures on the roof. (sg)

Sellwood Cycle Repair   *7639 SE Milwaukie Ave / 503-233-9292 / Tu-Sa 10-6* Conveniently located near the southern terminus OMSI-Springwater trail. New and used bike sales and service, one of the best places in town to buy a good used bike. Website has a lot of nice old bicycle posters on it (sg)

Seven Corners Cycle and Fitness   *2314 SE Division St / 503-245-9744* Friendly shop offering bicycle sales and service.

Veloce Bicycles   *3202 SE Hawthorne Blvd / 503-234-8400* Shop specializing in new road and city bicycle sales, plus consignment bicycles and bicycle fitting. (sg)

Veloshop *211 Sw 9th Ave / 503-335-Velo (8356) / Mo-Fr 10-6 Sa 12-4* Originally in Northeast, this nifty shop moved down into the "Indie-Rock-Block" last year. Velo offers reasonably priced sales and service. Woman owned, and supports women racers. They also sell their own lycra racing apparel. Instead of the corporate logos on most racing clothing, Velo's outfit has locally owned business sponsors. (sg)

(sl)

Weir's Cyclery *8247 N Lombard St / 503-283-3883 / Mo-Sa 10a-7p, Su 12a-5p* Weir's is Portland's oldest bicycle shop (since 1925!) and has been owned the Weir family from the start. Weir's specializes in "regular" (road, mountain, etc) bike sales and service and also features BMX and skateboards. Sadly, the original Weir's location at 5036 N Lombard St is no more, the current location in St Johns opened in 2007 after moving down the street from their 2003 spot. (sg)

Bicycle Resources

You can find various bicycle maps at Portland's local bicycle shops, or also at the Bicycle Transportation Alliance office (717 SW 12th Ave. 503.226.0676 Tu-Fr 9-5). You can also get them direct this-a-way:

City of Portland bike commuter map and Downtown bike map (free)-Call: 503-823-CYCL.

City of Portland Family-friendly Bicycle maps for Southeast, North, Northeast, and Outer Southeast Portland (free)- call 503-823-CYCL.

Multnomah County bike map and brochure (free)- call 503-988-5050

Oregon Coast Bike Route map, Oregon Bicycling Guide (statewide bicycle route map), Columbia River Gorge bike map (free)- call 503-823-CYCL.

Springwater Corridor Map (free) from Portland Parks & Recreation: 503-823-2223

Bike There, a bicycle map of the metropolitan area ($6.00, this one costs ya but is pretty durn good) call 503-797-1900

Additionally, many of the free city maps can be obtained directly from the Portland Office of Transportation, 1120 SW Fifth (in the Portland Building), Room 800 (normal business hours) (sg)

Regular Bikey Events

This is no way, shape or form a comprehensive list of bicycle events in and around Portland. This list concentrates mostly on alt-bike culture stuff that happens regularly. For more in-depth listings, go to: http://www.bta4bikes.org/act/calendar.html (the Bicycle Transportation Alliance calendar) or http://calendar.shifttobikes.org (the Shift calendar)

Weekly

SUNDAY, 9am: Woman's Bike Ride. Meet at Bike Gallery, 5329 NE Sandy. 20-30 mile ride, no one left behind.

SUNDAY, 5pm: Women's Volunteer Night. Meet at Community Cycling Center, 1700 NE Alberta St. The shop is open to women for an opportunity to learn bike maintenance and tool use in an extra supportive environment under the guidance of our female staff. (NOTE: must first attend Wed. Volunteer Orientation)

SUNDAY, 8pm: ZOOBOMB. Meet between 8 and 9p. See Zoobomb listing in "Who's Who" for more info.

TUESDAY, 6-8:30pm: Volunteer Night at North Portland Bikeworks. 3951 N Mississippi Ave. Learn bike repair skills, earn volunteer credit hours.

TUESDAY, 7-9pm: Volunteer Night at the Community Cycling Center. 1700 NE Alberta. (NOTE: must first attend Wed. Volunteer Orientation)

WEDNESDAY, 6-8pm: Woman's Bike Repair Night at North Portland Bikeworks. 3951 N Mississippi Ave. Free workshops open to all who identify as women (trans friendly).

Bike Polo (es)

Learn about bike repair either on bikes at the shop or by fixing your own bike!

WEDNESDAY, 7-9pm: Volunteer Orientation and Volunteer Night at the Community Cycling Center. 1700 NE Alberta St.

Monthly

SECOND FRIDAY OF THE MONTH: Do you like riding your bikes at night? How would you like to do that with a group of folks? How 'bout throw some surprises into the mix? Then check out the Midnight Mystery Ride. The meet-up occurs at a local bar between 11pm to midnight. At the stroke of 12, the ride departs, but where does it go? A-ha, only the ride leader knows! The group traverses the city streets for 1 to 5 miles, and ends up at a secret location. Check out http://www.yeabikes.net/midnight/ for the meeting location of the upcoming ride, and also to learn how you, yes YOU, can lead your own ride!

LAST FRIDAY OF THE MONTH, 7-9am: Do you bicycle commute to work, but don't have any time to eat or, gasp, have coffee on the way? Don't fear, brave bicyclist, help is on the way! Breakfast on the Bridges provides FREE coffee and pastries to those riding to downtown from the eastside. Stop a couple minutes, chat with fellow bicyclists, and refresh. Oh, don't worry about being late to work! Breakfast on the Bridges regularly occurs on the Hawthorne and Broadway bridges, but may be expanded to the Steel bridge soon. To learn more, or to volunteer, email timolandia@ShiftToBikes.org or check the Shift calendar.

LAST FRIDAY OF THE MONTH, 5:30pm: Critical Mass. See listing in "Who's Who" for more info.

SOMETIME EACH MONTH: Slug Velo. A friendly, leisurely ride group that has organized monthly rides, all emphasizing fun. Each ride is a unique, 10-20 mile cycling adventure. No one is left behind. Perfect for beginning cyclists and those who don't always want to get somewhere in a hurry. Go to the Shift calendar or www.slugvelo.com for info. (NOTE: Helmets and lights – if ride is at night – required. May be asked to sign a waiver for participation.)

Annually or Ir-regularly

USUALLY MONTHLY: An Urban Adventure League ride. See "Who's Who" for more info.

(nb)

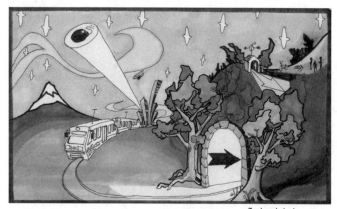

Zoobomb (es)

EASTER SUNDAY: Bunny on a Bike Ride. Led by Carye Bye of Red Bat Press, this ride playfully celebrates the holiday. Ride around dress up (or not dressed up) as a bunny for 3-5 miles, finding hidden treasures along the way! For more info, go to www.redbatpress.com

SOMETIME IN JUNE: Pedalpalooza (Bikesummer). Portland's annual celebration of bikey fun! Basically a continuation of Bikesummer 2002, this is a two-plus week celebration of bicycles, with events coming in from different sources. The 2004 Pedalpalooza contained almost 70 events, which is roughly the same amount that happened in Bikesummer 2002, but in half the time! The grand finale is the Multnomah County Bike Fair, a cycling take on the traditional country fair. Previous fairs have had a midway, music, and events such as Eating Contest (where contestants had to eat while riding!), Slow Bike Race, Jousting, Bike Rodeo and Derby. Pedalpalooza is facilitated by Shift, see their website and calendar for more info: www.shifttobikes.org

SOMETIME IN SUMMER: Chunkathalon. See Chunk 666 listing in "Who's Who".

JULY/AUGUST: Rose Pedal. This multi-week event is the culmination of mainstreamy bike culture (it's sponsored by Providence Health Care). Many different events, most family friendly, most cost $$$. There are two highlights: Everybody Bikes, at the beginning, where bicyclists get free or discounted admission to various cultural institutions (though the time window is very limited), and the Bridge Pedal, a massive (2004's was over 15,000 riders!) ride over most of Portland's Bridges (which there is a lot of.) This is the only time you can (legally) ride over the freeway bridges, Marquam and Fremont.

www.providence.org/oregon/events/rose_pedal/default.htm (sg)

Useful Tips and Advice for Bicycling in Portland

LOCK YOUR BIKE! Bike thievery is a big problem here. Even leaving your bike unguarded for "just a sec" could mean it gone forever. Invest in a good U-Lock (one that preferably can't be opened by a Bic pen) and when locking make sure you have at least one wheel and part of the frame inside the lock. Remove anything from the bike one can take-especially lights!

USE LIGHTS AT NIGHT. It's safe and it's the law. Portland cops are good at busting you for not having one at night, especially at Critical Mass. (Yes, they have even arrested peeps for not having a light at Mass!) Oregon law requires a bicycle must have a white light visible at least 500 feet from the front, and a red light or reflector visible at least 600 feet from the rear.

WATCH OUT FOR THE TRACKS! PDX has many railroad and streetcar tracks that criss-cross the town. The story of an unsuspected bicyclist "biting it" when encountering the rails is heard far too often here. Don't get hurt and have to go to the hospital! Hospital trips suck for the uninsured! To avoid injury, ALWAYS cross tracks at as close to a right angle as possible. Slow down when crossing. Be especially careful when it's wet out. And know your bike: fatter, mountain bike tires handle tracks and road imperfections better than thin road tires. Also to note: it is perfectly legal to ride on the left side of a one-way street, so you can avoid the tracks on SW/NW 10th and 11th in that way.

DON'T RIDE ON THE SIDEWALKS DOWNTOWN. While it is legal to sidewalk ride in other areas of the city, it is not legal downtown. "Downtown" is roughly defined as the area hemmed in by the Willamette, I-405, and NW Lovejoy St. Cops like to ticket on this one, too.

DON'T RIDE IN THE "BUS ONLY" LANE IN THE TRANSIT MALL DOWNTOWN, either. (The transit mall is located on SW/NW 5th and 6th Aves) Yeah, it's a stupid law, but one the Portland Police have been especially vigilant on. The only consolation to give if you get ticketed for this offense is: you aren't alone. Also, don't ride in the "bus only" lanes in the Rose Quarter Transit Center, or you may face the same consequences. The fuzz have been cracking down here as well.

MOST OF THE WILLAMETTE RIVER BRIDGES ARE CROSSABLE, except for the Marquam and Fremont (both freeway crossings). The most bike-friendly ones are the Hawthorne, Burnside, Steel (both decks!) and Broadway. The Hawthorne and Broadway have sidewalk bicycle lanes that connect to bicycle routes on either side of the river. The Steel has a walkway on the lower deck that connects the Waterfront Park path (westside) with the Eastbank Esplanade. The Burnside has bike lanes on the bridge, but has poor connections off the bridge. While you can legally cross the four other Willamette spans (Sellwood, Ross Island, Morrison, St. Johns), none of them have good bike facilities.

Of note is the Morrison Bridge. While its central location would be great for a bicycle crossing, it really sucks to have to use this bridge. For one, bicycles are prohibited from the roadway and must stay on the sidewalk. And using the sidewalk means using three separate series of stairs (up and down) to go around all the highway on-ramps. This sucks for pedestrians also Sometime in the near future the Morrison will become more bicycle and pedestrian friendly, until then, use one of the other bridges instead.

The two Columbia River spans into Vancouver, Wash, the Interstate (I-5) and the Glenn Jackson (I-205) are bike crossable as well, if you get the jonesin' to head for the 'couv. Tip: it's better to use the Glenn Jackson bridge southbound, because the northbound trip is long and uphill. (sg)

Bicycle Advocacy, Culture, and Fun

C.H.U.N.K. 666 C.H.U.N.K. 666 is hard to explain, so I'll let their website speak for them: "We are a bicycle club and temperance league. We are a wandering klezmer band working to hasten the heat death of the universe...Most importantly, we are believers in the use of muscle-powered steeds which augment the physiology of their riders. After the imminent Apocalypse, gasoline and bullets will be rare. Those who already ride bicycles and shoot bb guns and slingshots today will easily dominate the huddled masses tomorrow." The devotees of the Chunk can be seen riding around town on their custom built "choppers", sometimes in packs. Every summer, they host the Chunkathalon, which is a series of contests including powerslide competition, baby rescue, the gauntlet, flaming wall of death, and "tall bike" jousting championships. 2004's happened on September 11th (go figure). (sg)

Critical Mass   *meet-up spot is in the North Park Blocks at NW Couch St. and NW Park Ave. (look for the big elephant)*
Critical Mass occurs every last Friday of the month at 5:30pm. The meet-up spot is in the North Park Blocks at NW Couch St. and NW Park Ave. (look for the big elephant). Ride with a big group of people (sometimes 1,000+ !!) around town "en masse" to demonstrate that bicycles have as much right to use the streets as cars.

The police presence at the Mass has been overbearing ever since the August 2002 ride, when police made dozens of arrests. The cops are using "divide and conquer" tactics to neutralize the effectiveness of the ride. If you want

(ar)

to ride, be prepared for police harassment. The Portland Police in the past HAVE arrested and THROWN PEOPLE FROM THEIR MOVING BICYCLES for simple violations as running a YELLOW light and NOT HAVING A BICYCLE LIGHT. Make sure you bring working lights!!

Due to the severe legal harrasement, Critical Mass has lost a lot of steam in Portland. But a new crop of Massers hope to re-invigorate the mass. They actually managed to get our new mayor Tom Potter to ride the mass in January 2005, the first time our mayor has done so. Consequently, the police have gotten tamer, though there still has been ticketing and no one seems to like the overbearing motorcycle cops.

SHIFT Born out of Portland's Bikesummer 2002, Shift is a bicycle advocacy organization working to promote Portland's creative bike culture and highlight bicycling's positive contributions to the community. They plan, execute, publicize, and/or have a hand in an ever-widening variety of bike-related events. There is no membership list, fee, or dues to be a part of it. Their website features an extensive calendar of bike related events. (sg)

Urban Adventure League *PO Box 14185, Portland, OR 97293-0185 / http://urbanadventureleague.blogspot.com* The Urban Adventure League aims to reconnect you to your "childlike sense of wonder". The "league" hosts various events that explores the urban environment using bicycles and other non-auto forms of getting around. All Urban Adventure League sponsored events and projects emphasize fun, de-emphasize competition, and foster connectivity and awareness. Boredom will not be allowed. The league isn't really a club or organization, but if you would like to become an "Official Member" of it, or learn more about what they do and when they do it, email urbanadventureleague@scribble.com

Zoobomb Is it a cult? Or a way of life? Whatever it may be, Zoobomb is fun. The deal: every Sunday night a gang of bike-folks meets up at Rocco's Pizza (949 SW Oak St, at intersection of W Burnside, SW 10th Ave, and SW Oak) between 8 and 9pm. At 9, everyone takes their bike (or one of the bikes provided) to the nearest MAX station to catch a train to the Washington Park-Zoo Station. They ride from the station to the top of the hill, hang out a bit at a "secret" location, and then "bomb" down the steep, winding road through the park back down to the Civic Stadium, I mean, PGE Park station. This is usually repeated a few times, with refreshing done at the top. Fun! The initiated ride children's bikes (referred to as "little" bikes) which are piled up on the bike racks near Rocco's.

As with many activities in this vein, Zoobomb has felt the heat of, well "the heat". Tri-Met fare inspectors like to give them grief (a note to the wise: ALWAYS pay the $1.65 fare if you plan on riding the MAX to Zoobomb, otherwise you might end up with a ticket for fare evasion!), the neighborhood association around the Zoo has been at odds with them (going as far as to try to get the MAX station to close early on Sunday nights), and even the Department of Homeland Security considered them a possible "terrorist threat" at one point!! But things have mellowed out a bit for now. (sg)

Portland Bicycling Facilities

Portland is one of the few North American cities that really cares about bicycle facilities-meaning that they just don't pay lip service to improving the plight of the bicyclist, they actually spend money on it. Of course, Portland is nowhere near perfect, and still needs more work. If you subscribe to the Effective Cycling philosophy, you'd probably argue against spending money on bike facilities. But here is what we've got:

Bicycle (multi-use) Paths/Trails (Class I): These are bikeways that are totally separated from motorized traffic. These facilities are where you'll see the most "recreational" or weekend bicyclists. There aren't that many in Portland, the longer ones being close to the Willamette (Waterfront Park, Eastbank Esplanade, OMSI-Springwater) or Columbia (Marine Drive, Columbia Slough) rivers. The longest is the Springwater Corridor in far SE Portland. See "Where to Ride" for more info

Bike Lanes (Class II): These are marked lanes on streets, exclusively for the use of bicycles. Bike lanes are generally found on higher-traffic streets in town. Portland has a quite extensive system of bike lanes in comparison to other Western cities. While it can be argued that bicycle lanes can do more harm than good (poorly engineered, danger from right-turning traffic, promotes bad bicycling habits, etc), we got 'em, people use 'em, and they aren't as poorly designed as bike lanes in some cities. However, it's highly annoying when a bike lane abruptly ends on a busy street and you have to scramble for safety.

One of the cooler things about bicycle lanes in town is that some of the "international symbol for bicyclist" type street paintings have been altered. Some of them have mohawks, some are reading books, some are playing golf, etc. This has all been done by clever Dept. of Transportation street painters. Probably the best example of this can be found on NW Broadway, between W Burnside and NW Hoyt.

Bicycle Boulevards (Class III): These are low traffic through streets designated by the Dept of Transportation as bike ways. Many of them feature traffic-calming devices such as street islands and speed bumps, and some of them have special traffic lights to aid bicyclists (and pedestrians) in crossing busy streets. The only problem is that you really need a map to figure out where these routes are. Signing is spotty, generally the generic "Bike Route" sign will be found with little else. Route-specific signage with Boulevard names, directions, and distance (seen in Vancouver BC and Berkeley CA) are still a ways away. (sg)

Fun Places to Ride Your Bicycle in Portland

Most anywhere in Portland is a good place to ride! As long as you avoid some of the busier thoroughfares and know how to get where you're going effectively (a bike map sure does come in handy!), you'll have fun bicycling around town. But there are some areas that are more of a destination for cyclists (especially recreational cyclists). Most of them are because of the state of the bicycle facility (bike paths), while some are because of the scenery. So here are some of the more travelled ones:

The Springwater Corridor: This is the longest of Portland's bicycle paths, and also one of the first. This linear park/multi-use path starts on the east edge of the Sellwood neighborhood in the SE and goes all the way to the exotic town of Boring (yes, that IS its real name.) This route was originally an interurban streetcar line. The length of the path is approximately 16 miles long , and the main entrance (trailhead) is at SE 45th at SE Johnson Creek Blvd. In the future, this trail will fully connect to the OMSI-Springwater Trail (see Oaks Bottom listing) via a series of bridges spanning 99E, the UP railroad tracks, and Johnson Creek. When that happens, we'll have a 21-mile long path, reaching from downtown Portland to Boring! Until then, you'll have to use a somewhat-tricky street connection via SE Spokane St to get between the two.

It has been argued that the Springwater isn't particularly scenic, and parts of it definitely are not. And its distance from downtown--a good 5 miles to get there--makes this a destination, not a connection between two points. But there's enough interesting stuff along the way to make it worthwhile, like Tideman-Johnson Park, Powell Butte, Leach Botanical Gardens, Beggars-Tick Wildlife Reserve, the farmlands and open spaces east of I-205, and the great views of Mount Hood.

Eastbank Esplanade: This path runs along the east bank of the Willamette River between the Steel and Hawthorne Bridges. There are some cool historical markers along the route. And the 1,200 ft. long floating walkway (just north of the Burnside Bridge) is the longest floating walkway in the United States. This path is heavily used by pedestrians, rollerbladers, and others, and can get crowded on weekend. The Eastbank connects to the Waterfront Park paths via Steel and Hawthorne Bridges.

Waterfront Park Path: This linear greenway lies along the west bank of the Willamette River between the Steel and Hawthorne Bridges. This is the most heavily used path in town, on weekends during summer it becomes super-congested, making riding through a chore. But it is the place to see and be seen!

(es)

Willamette River Path (West Side): This is a paved multi-use path that runs through Willamette Park, connecting it to the Sellwood Bridge and the SW Industrial district. This trail is less "natural" than the OMSI-Springwater path on the east bank, as it passes through several apartment and business complexes (and can get quite choked with traffic at times). The engineering isn't that great, either, as there are many sharp 90° turns to navigate. To access the trail is a bit tricky; the best way from downtown is to take the Waterfront Path south of the Hawthorne Bridge through the condominium nonsense and under the Marquam Bridge. Then continue on SW Moody Ave through the warehouse district (watch the railroad tracks!) and find the trailhead near an espresso stand. You can also use the Sellwood Bridge to connect to OMSI-Springwater (and make a big loop of the river!) NOTE: Due to construction in this area, it may be more difficult to access the northern end of the path. In the future, the bicycle path will fully connect to Waterfront Park.

OMSI-Springwater Path: This paved multi-use path parallels the old Portland Traction (interurban) rail line. This path connects the Eastbank Esplanade south of the Hawthorne Bridge and passes by the Oregon Museum of Science and Industry. It then goes on-road until it becomes a path on SE 4th Ave. south of SE Division Place by the Ross Island Bridge (watch out for all the Ross Island cement trucks!) It then runs all the way south to the Sellwood Bridge at SE Spokane St, cutting through Oaks Bottom Wildlife Refuge. It's a good place to ride fast and long. If you need a quick connection from Sellwood to downtown via bike, this is it! Make sure you check out the gi-normous blue heron mural on the wall of the mausoleum (look across the pond from the trail.

Along the Columbia River and Slough: The Slough area is a weird mix of riparian forest, marshland, heavy industry, and things that the rest of the city doesn't want to see (landfills, jails, airports, etc.) You can be going by a tranquil pond one minute, then an auto junkyard the next. The Columbia Slough has always been Portland's dumping ground, out of sight, out of mind. That said, there is still some cool nature down there, and bicycling along the slough can be an enjoyable experience. There are several bike paths or lanes paralleling the major east-west thoroughfare, Marine Drive. From NE 33rd Ave to the I-205 Bridge at 112 Ave, the bike path only crosses a road once, so it's a great place to ride fast and long. Watch out though, the paths along the Slough provide little in cover, so you'll get baked by the sun in the summer. The other major drawback to riding around the Slough is that its bike paths are not connected that well, so you may have to make some tricky connections along busy, truck-dominated roads. But the bike path network is expanding every year, so one day you'll be able to ride peacefully from Kelley Point Park on the western tip to Troutdale at the gates of the Columbia Gorge!

Terwilliger Boulevard: This is a linear park that starts from the south end of downtown and winds through the west hills all the way to I-5. It isn't closed to cars, but the street has marked bike lanes and traffic is generally peaceful. The whole boulevard is tree-lined, so you'll keep shaded while pumping up and down the hills along the route. Catch a glimpse of Portland below where the foliage breaks let you. Note all the joggers that use the route. South of the I-5 underpass, the Boulevard becomes a standard street with bike lanes, but south of Boones' Ferry Road, there is a separated bike path that runs all the way to Lake Oswego through the forested slopes of Tyron Creek State Park. The problem if you head all the way to Oswego is that there's no place to go but back, since any other route outta that burg sucks for bikes. (Use EXTREME caution if you decide to bike back to Portland along Oregon 43-Riverside Drive!)

The West Hills: A great place to ride if you like to get a workout and take in the view of Portland below! Ride up to Council Crest, the highest point in the city at 1070 feet (325 meters) via SW Montgomery Drive. Wind along Skyline Drive, dodging all the fast cars along the way! "Bomb" down Marquam Hill through the OHSU craziness!

Mount Tabor: At 650 feet (200 meters), Mount Tabor is one of the highest points on the east side, and a great place to ride. And it's an extinct volcano! Some of the roads on the hill are closed to automotive traffic (all roads closed to cars on Wednesdays) Huff and puff up to the top and take in the view! Don't get intimidated by all the road bikers beating you to the top!

Rocky Butte: This hidden gem of a hill in the Northeast offers a good bicycle workout, and the best viewpoint on the eastside! Get an almost 360° panorama from the top of this volcanic cinder cone, and see downtown; the west hills; Washington State; the Columbia River; the gateway to the Gorge; the scary eastern metropolitan hinterlands, Mount Hood, St Helens, Adams, and Jefferson; and the best view of the airport in town! Come up the hill using the north route, and descend using the south route, going through the secret Rocky Butte Tunnel!

Laurelhurst, Ladds Addition, Irvington, Alameda: These quiet neighborhoods on the eastside, with their upper-income-bracket housing, offer great places to bicycle in peace.

I-205 Bike Path/I-84 Bike Path: I've included these two along-freeway bicycle paths in here for the sake of completeness. Both were built in the 1970's or so, before bike path engineering was "perfected", so they are both poorly engineered routes. The I-205 route has several crossings of busy boulevards, with no good way of crossing them. The I-84 path is right alongside the freeway, with only a concrete barrier separating you from traffic. Plus, they are both have lousy scenery (unless you like looking at freeways), and are on the eastern outer edge of town, so they don't really go anywhere (unless you are using the I-205 path to connect to the Springwater Corridor or Marine Drive paths).

Forest Park: Most of Forest Park is off-limits to bicyclists, since many trails are narrow, steep, and easily eroded. Besides a couple firelanes, the main place to bicycle is Leif Erickson Drive. This dirt road starts at the end of NW Thurman St and winds along the hills for 11 miles before terminating at NW Germantown Road, about a mile west of the

St. Johns Bridge. The Drive is fairly level, with few steep hills, but it definitely meanders. And it's better suited for moutain bikes, since there's lots of rock on the roadway. But it's a great place to bicycle in the near-wilderness for hours, if you want a different cycling experience! For maps of Forest Park, go to

www.portlandparks.org/NaturalAreas/Forest.htm

Willamette Boulevard: This street in North Portland begins at N Interstate Ave, one block south of Killingsworth. It cuts westward through residential neighborhoods until it hits Mocks Crest overlooking Swan Island and Mocks Bottom. From there, it follows the bluff, giving great views of the industrial city below and the West Hills across the river. There are bike lanes on Willamette Blvd between N Portland Blvd and N Ida St (at the railroad cut). From there you can continue north to the St Johns-Cathedral Park neighborhoods. Or use the Peninsula Crossing Trail, a separated path that connects to the Columbia Slough network of trails, via the railroad cut. (sg)

City Repair

Imagine this: You're cruising on your cruiser through the sunny Sunnyside neighborhood one sunshiney summer day. You're rolling eastward along SE Yamhill Street, letting the gentle grip of gravity propel you down the shallow hill from SE 30th. As you approach the intersection of SE 33rd Ave, your eyes are caught by a bright mass of yellow plopped in the middle of the street. As you get closer, you notice the yellow is actually a giant sunflower painted onto the asphalt at the intersection! You stop in your tracks, puzzled.

Memorial Lifehouse (sg)

Then you notice that on each corner, there are large orange barrels with a wire sunflower growing out of it! And even curioser, on the NE corner, there's a small waterfall in someone's yard, and a community messageboard constructed of--strawbale? This is the part where you say to yourself: "What the hell's going on here?" City Repair is what's going on here. What's City Repair, you may ask? "The City Repair Project is group of citizen activists creating public gathering places and helping others to creatively transform the places where they live" is what their website says. In plainer English, they are trying to bring back the public square, which has been long-dead (or was it stillborn?) in American urban planning. Since most of the U.S. (at least west of the Mississippi) is based on the grid system with its rigid traffic-only intersections, there's really no public place, save for parks, for people to meet and hang out. City Repair works with neighborhoods to repair intersections that will allow people, and maybe even leprechauns, to come together in a public space, meet their neighbors, communicate, share, and the like. The most visible manifestation of what they do is through two projects: Intersection Repair, and The Village Building Convergence. Traversing the town, you may see some of the cool things City Repair is responsible for, or has a hand in. Their office is located at 2126 SE Division St. (sg)

Labrynth Piazza in Buckman   *Intersection of SE Washington St. and SE 19th Av* Built in 2003, this repair is happening in the oft-ignored Buckman. Look for the labrynth painted on the street (admittedly more subtle and not as obvious as the Share-it or Sunnyside paintings.) A cob kiosk and tiled bench can be found near the SW corner. (sg)

Memorial Lifehouse   *SE corner of SE Taylor St. and SE 37th Av* On May 27, 1998, 27-year old Matthew Schekel was riding his bicycle down Taylor when a delivery truck ran a stop-sign on 37th, hitting and killing Matthew. After the accident, an impromptu memorial sprung up, two bicycle frames covered in flowers put into the dirt between sidewalk and street. In spring of 2002, City Repair built a more permanent installation. Getting the permission of the property owner at the corner, they built a "Memorial Lifehouse" directly into the retaining wall here. Made out of cob, the lifehouse has an "ecoroof", covered with plants that will absorb rainwater. At the base of the lifehouse is an alcove for random trinkets and other ephemera in tribute of Matthew. To the right is a bench covered in intricate glass mosaic and stonework. At the right end is a solar panel/bicycle wheel atop another tower. Planted into the lawn is a wheel with an account of Matthew's life and the project that brought this wonderful structure into being. I always pause when I ride by here, and reflect on the beauty of he memorial, and on how one stupid mistake can end someone's life. (sg)

Seven Corners Intersection Repair   *Intersection of SE Ladd Ave, SE 20th Ave, SE 21st Ave, and SE Division St* It's called "Seven Corners" because of all the different streets intersecting here (of course!) What you'll find is a cob information kiosk outside the Red and Black Café (see separate listing) at SE Division and SE 22nd, plus new cob benches in front of the Mirador store. (sg)

Share-it Square *Intersection of SE Sherrett St. and SE 9th Ave* This intersection repair was the first project City Repair worked on, way back in the dark ages of 1996. On the NE corner you'll find a community bulletin board, picnic table, a li'l stove shaped like a beehive, and a trade station where peeps can drop off or pick up produce, household items, etc. On the SW Corner, there is a "24 hour Tea Station" which provides free tea supposedly 24-7 via an airpot, plus a beautifu cob bench. On the NW corner, there's a small open "house" with toys for kids and various books and magazines to peruse while you're hanging out here. And in the intersection itself is painted a big bullseye-esque pattern. (sg)

Share-it Square (km)

Sunnyside Piazza *Intersection of SE Yamhill St. and SE 33rd Av* This intersection saw its repairing begin in late 2001 with the painting of the sunflower. Since then, the most noticeable building has occurred on its NE corner, with the message kiosk (with a solar-powered light!) and solar-powered fountain. There are also some yellow rainbarrels on the corner of this intersection. Check out the cool Victorian houses here as well. (sg)

Museums

Cultural Pass We haven't talked about most of the museums in town basically because of how expensive they are (The Portland Art Museum can cost you $10-15). Costly museum admissions are not Zinester's Guide approved. There is a way, however, to circumnaviagate said fees. And that is through the Cultural Pass. The Cultural Pass allows free access to a number of Portland area museums and institutions. You can reserve a pass through one of the area libraries. There are several catches, though:

1) You must be a Portland area resident

2) No Multnomah County library offers this service, just Washington and Clackamas counties

3) You must pick up and return the pass on the same day, fines are as steep as $5 a day for a late pass

4) If you lose the pass, you must buy a new one, and they generally run about $100

The best area library to pick up a pass from is the Lake Oswego Library. This library offers the best hours, so you can pick up your pass quite early and get the most out of it. The library is located at 706 4th St in Lake Oswego (about eight miles south of downtown Portland), and is a couple block walk from the Lake Oswego Transit Center. Tri-Met bus lines #35/Macadam and #40/John's Landing provide service from downtown Portland. Call 503-636-7628 for library hours, pass conditions, and to reserve a pass. They have passes for Portland Art Museum, the Children's Garden, Japanese Garden, Chinese Classical Gardens, and Pittock Mansion. (sg)

Hiking In and Around Portland by Paul Nama

In addition to a very rich city life, Portland is situated amidst amazing geography. Within 100 miles of Portland one can see almost any type of climate or structure, some of which can be viewed without even leaving the city.

The west hills of Portland offer miles of interesting hiking trails that are accessible at various points by bus or max. At over 30 miles in length, the Wildwood trail weaves its way through the west hills connecting Hoyt Arboretum and Washighton Park to Forest Park. The trail starts a few hundred yards up the hill from the Washington Park/zoo max stop (served by the blue line and some extended red line trains). Following the Wildwood trail you will pass a viewpoint where Mt. St. Helens is visible on a clear day. Between 1.75 and 2 miles down the Wildwood Trail is another trail that leads to the Japanese Garden. Look carefully from above and you can see parts of the Japanese Garden without paying the hefty entrance fee. Below the Japanese Garden is the Rose Garden, which supports a world famous collection of different breeds of roses. Continuing downhill is Washington Park and a fine city view, before ending up back in town. The Wildwood trail is clearly marked, and since it is all downhill no maps are necessary to find your way back into the city. On the north side of Washington park you can catch the #20 Burnside bus back to downtown, or cross the street into the swanky northwest neighborhood for the 15, 17 or Portland Streetcar.

Built in 1914 by Henry Pittock, founder of the Oregonian, the Pittock Mansion is near the four mile mark of the Wildwood Trail. For the interior design oriented folks there is a tour of the house, but the real attraction is the backyard ($5.50

for the home tour, backyard is free). From the backyard all of Portland can be seen, and on a clear day Mt. Hood completes the horizon (through the trees Mt. St. Helens and Mt. Rainier can also be seen). There are benches and a picnic tale in the backyard, and this is a fine place to have lunch or take a break. There is a restroom and a drinking fountain at Pittock Mansion, but you will need to pack in your own lunch as they do not sell lunch there.

Coming down the hill from Pittock Mansion (the trail continues in the back of the parking lot), the Wildwood trail goes downhill for about two miles before connecting with the Lower MacLeay trail. This section is steep as it traverses through the forested canyons of the west hills. (There are many trails not described here that end in various West Hills neighborhoods.) After crossing Balch Creek, the Wildwood Trail intersects with the Lower MacLeay trail, which leads down the creek to MacLeay Park. MacLeay Park starts at NW 29th and Thurman, which is accessible via the #15 bus.

Instead of going all the way on the Wildwood trail, the shorter path to Pittock mansion is to cross through Hoyt Arboretum, picking up the Wildwood trail near the three mile mark. The first and 3rd mile of the Wildwood trail go through the Hoyt Arboretum, which covers 175 acres and contains plant life from around the world. There are posted maps as well as a map for sale in the visitor center. Trails are clearly marked, and depending on what you want to see or how far you want to walk you can create any hike in the arboretum. Personally, I like the redwoods, although they are not as big as those found near the coast south of Portland.

The hikes between MacLeay Park and the start of the Wildwood Trail can be more or

(km)

less difficult depending on which direction they are walked in. The Washington Park max stop is about 710 feet above sea level; Pittock Mansion is about 950 feet above sea level; points in town (MacLeay Park, Burnside & NW 23rd) are probably about 100 feet above sea level. As such, starting in MacLeay Park and going up to Pittock mansion would be the most challenging way to experience this trail system, whereas hiking from the start of the Wildwood trail back to town is all downhill and much less strenuous. None of these trails are flat, so expect gentle grades constantly.

If you have access to a car the ocean or Mt. St. Helens are less than 2 hours from Portland. Less than 1 hour to the east is the Columbia River Gorge, which is home to amazing geologic formations, breathtaking waterfalls, and endless hiking opportunities. The easiest way to tour the gorge is to take I-84 east to exit 35, where you can pick up the Historic Columbia River Highway (HCRH) going back west. Continuing west on the scenic highway (HCRH) is Horsetail Falls, Multnomah Falls, Wahkeena Falls, Latourell falls, and Crown Point Vista House (among many other destinations) before ending near Troutdale, east of Portland. Maps and hiking advice are available 7 days per week from the Friends of Multnomah Falls in the visitor center at Multnomah Falls.

The trailhead at Horsetail Falls leads back to Ponytail Falls, where the trail actually crosses behind the waterfall before continuing on to Oneonta Gorge; beyond the bridge over the gorge about 1.4 miles is Triple Falls. The elevation there is about 700 feet (trailhead is probably close to 100 feet above sea level), making this five mile out-and-back a moderate hike with a lot of spectacular things to see. Keep an eye out for Bigfoot as you hike the northwest, especially as Bigfoot's main stomping ground, Skamania County, is only a few miles down the river on the Washington side of the gorge.

Oneonta gorge is also accessible via the scenic highway. There is a cool waterfall in the gorge, but it is only accessible by hiking one mile up the gorge. Since this hike requires wading through Oneonta creek it is only recommended on a hot summer day, where you will probably encounter swarms of humanity with the same idea...

The next good hiking opportunity starts at Multnomah falls. Multnomah Falls is the tallest in the gorge (2nd highest continuously flowing waterfall in the nation at 620 feet) and has the largest crowds. The first 1.25 miles of this trail (441) sucks because it is paved and crowded and very steep with no real view, but the country above Multnomah Falls is beautiful and less crowded. From the Top of Multnomah falls the Larch Mountain Trail (441) covers 6.6 miles and 4000 feet from Multnomah lodge to the top of Larch Mountain. A more moderate loop is available, following trail 420 (off 441 about one mile past the top of Multnomah

Falls) across a ridge to Wahkeena springs and back down to Wahkeena Falls, where a connection trail (442) returns to Multnomah Falls. This loop covers rapids, five big waterfalls, and some nice gorge views over 5.5 miles (highpoint ~1600 feet above sea level). To add more to this loop follow trail 420C up to Devil's Rest. Here the crowd thins out even more (99% of the crowd does not go beyond the top of Multnomah Falls) and provides some nice views over the 3.2 mile out-and-back which peaks near 2400 feet above sea level. The Multnomah Falls area can also be accessed directly by exit 31 off I-84.

Continuing west on the scenic highway near exit 28 is the Angel's Rest Trailhead. This hike covers ~2.5 miles to ~1600 feet elevation. Along the way you will see Coopey Falls, and at the top you will find an amazing gorge view and a nice place to eat lunch. This trail is best on a calm, clear day, as the top is not protected and can be very windy.

At exit 28 there is westbound freeway access, or continue west on the scenic highway to see Latourell Falls. This is not the tallest waterfall in the gorge (249 feet), but perhaps the most spectacular waterfall on the scenic highway. The trailhead leads to the top of the falls, and about one mile behind the falls is another waterfall. The trail leads over a bridge back to the other side of the top of Latourell Falls. From there the trail goes through some woods downhill, back across the scenic highway through a park, under an old concrete bridge, ending at the bottom of Latourell Falls. This loop is less strenuous than most gorge hikes, providing a favorable ratio of sights to exertion that is perfect for less ambitious hikers.

West of Latourell falls 2.5 miles is the Crown Point Vista House; there is no hiking here, but is is a great place to get out of the car and take in a nice view both east and west down the Columbia River. There is access to the freeway a few miles west in Corbett, or for a nice country drive stay on the scenic highway all the way to its end, near Troutdale. This tour could also be done in reverse by exiting I-84 at exit 22 and following the signs to the eastbound Historic Columbia River Highway.

There are so many places to visit in the gorge that they cannot all be mentioned here, but a few other points worth mentioning include Eagle Creek, Wahclella Falls, Bonneville Dam and fish hatchery, and the Bridge of the Gods. Located at exit 41 on I-84, the Eagle Creek Trail is perhaps the most popular and spectacular hike in the gorge. Most of the hike is on or above the creek, passing steep rock walls and numerous waterfalls (punchbowl @ 2.5 miles and tunnel falls at 6 miles are the biggest). Parking lots on the scenic highway are free, but parking at Eagle Creek (or its neighbor Wahclella) requires a Northwest Forest Pass (available at the Multnomah Falls gift shop or G.I. Joe's in town, $5 per day or $30 per year).

The Bonneville Dam is at exit 40. There is a visitor center at the dam with an underground view area where one can watch Salmon traverse the fish ladder in season. Near the dam is a shipping lock. No stop to this area is complete without going to the nearby fish hatchery to see the sturgeon. Sturgeon are prehistoric bottom feeders that get quite large, and the pool at the fish hatchery contains Herman the Sturgeon, who is 9' 7" long!

From the Bonneville Dam exit (40) on the south side of I-84 is the Wahclella Falls trailhead. This trial is about one mile long with a loop at the end, and is geographically similar to Eagle Creek. This trail is breathtaking and highly recommended for people with shorter hiking ranges. The gorge is nice to tour by car, but its true flavor is revealed to those who get out of the car and walk a little. Wahclella is a short and relatively flat, perfect for those whose health limits their ability to hike longer distances.

The town of Cascade Locks is at exit 44. This is significant because the Pacific Crest Trail crosses between Oregon and Washington on the Bridge of the Gods, so this could be used as a starting point for longer backpacking trips. There is a park in Cascade Locks (behind the ice cream place) where you can see the old lock. If you do not want to take I-84 back to Portland, cross the Bridge of the Gods and take Washington state route 14 west to I-205 southbound to Portland. This piece concentrated on the Oregon side of the gorge, but there are many hiking trails and excellent gorge views on the Washington side of the gorge.

Weather in Portland is generally rainy in the winter and sunny in the summer. All of the hikes described here are available in all seasons. Winter hiking can be wet, but waterfalls are generally bigger (and there are more small falls) in the rainy season. The Pacific Northwest is home to many types of wildflowers , which can be seen in the spring (especially at Dog Mountain on the Washington side of the gorge) on many hikes. Summer and fall can be less green but more comfortable; many trails change in character with the seasons.

Hopefully visitors and resident alike will take time to explore the variety of natural features that exist near Portland.

Skateboarding by Jered Bogli

One might think that given Oregon's rainy climate the skateboard scene would be as soggy as the weather. In fact the skate scene is one of the most vibrant in the country. Oregon and the rest of the Northwest has become the epicenter for a new skatepark building revolution. The DIY ethic of the Burnside skatepark served to launch this movement giving rise to two preminent skatepark design and build companies--Dreamland and Grindline--both having roots as the original crew responsible for the Burnside skatepark. Currently in Portland we have laws in place that give skateboarding the same treatment any other mode of transportation. What exactly that means is a little foggy. In part what it means is you have to obey the same traffic laws as any other vehicle. It also means you can skate all over downtown, however as usual many spots are a bust and despite the skating being legal you could say the legality of skating ends as soon as your wheels come off the ground. Locally there are a couple skateparks located close to downtown and countless others in the suburbs. Street spots tend to come and go quickly. The six months of rain and use of studded tires makes for some rough streets. Skating for transportation can be frustrating unless you have some big soft cruiser wheels, however the relatively small size of Portland combine with the usually temperate summer weather and a first class bus and rail system makes getting around the city on your board enjoyable and fairly efficient.

Burnside Skatepark (jm)

If you are looking for some new stuntwood while in town there are a number of shops to choose from depending on your estethic. Ah, the fashion of skate-boarding. Close in to downtown there are three major core skateshops. First off you have Cal Skate. Cal Skate is located at 210 NW 6th Ave. (503-248-0495, Mo- Fr 11a-6p, Sa 10a-6p Su 11a-5p, www.calsk8.com) The inside of Cal Skate is a veritable skate museum, old decks and skate ephemera lining all the walls. This shop is an institution here in town. Much goodness comes out of the shop and its employees who have their hands in most of what is happening in the Portland skate scene. This is the only shop of the three that ONLY stocks skate gear - talk about core! Next, also on the west side is Exit Real World located 206 NW 23rd St (between Burnside and Couch and across from Urban Outfitters). As you may have guessed given the chic location this is more of a high end botique shop, none the less the staff is quite friendly and helpful + they stock a whole lot of stuff and also tons of womens stuff being that the owner is a woman. Lastly going to the east side of the river is Cals Pharmacy (no relation to Cal Skate --donít ask!) at 1636 E Burnside St (503-233-1237). Image wise this shop falls neatly between Cal Skate and Exit. Not as dirty as Cal Skate, not as Squeaky clean as Exit. Buying a board here gives you a free session at The Department of Skateboarding which is part of the Pharmacy empire. The Department of skateboarding also has a fully stocked shop. There are more shops in town, but close in those are the main independent local players.

As for skateparks, under the east side of the Burnside bridge is the fabled DIY park that shares the same name as the bridge. The cement began being poured over ten years ago and the park continues to evolve thanks to the love and devotion of many of the original builders and some new recruits. Burnside has a reputation for being a rough place, however if you employ a bit of common sense youíll find that Burnside is quite friendly--a bit like a surly old grandfather or something. Learning how to skate Burnside is a lifelong process, so be forewarned. Some of the best times to show up and have a mellow session would be the early morning (although not allowed in the park the early morning is usually ruled by bikers), also around 10:30-12:30 usually affords a lull in the action and a time to learn a few lines. Once the hardcore locals start showing up it is best to find a good vantage point and watch the madness insue. If youíve got common sense you'll know when your time is up, sit back, watch and try to memorize a couple new lines for the next time. If you skate you must experience Burnside. Also close in to downtown at 15 NE Hancock (between N Vancouver Ave and NE MLK) is The Department of Skateboarding (503-493-9480) This is a pay to play indoor skatepark that features a fun 3' bowl with a wallride, an expansive and creative street course and a 6'-8' bowl in the back room. Sessions run $10 and a day pass for $15 (prices are lowered for members), but if you show up for the last hour they will charge you something like two to five dollars. You need to sign a waiver and have a helmet. I believe they have some rental helmets as well. You can find the schedule and download the waiver at (www.departmentofskateboarding.com).

Way up in North Portland located by the transit center in Pier Park (N. Seneca & St. Johns, off of N Lombard St) is the St. Johns Skatepark. This park is a giant turd, that being said if you want a mellow time and a good place to goof around a good time can be had here. The downside is via bus it will take forever to get here. This is about as far from downtown as you can get. (Accessible by the #40 Mocks Crest and #75 Lombard bus lines, the #75 can be picked up at the

Lombard stop on MAX-Yellow LIne)

If you're a vert dog you could head out to the crappy prefab park in Beaverton
(directions from max/26). The one redeeming quality is a solid vert ramp, which
may be the only vert ramp in the area. Unfortunately, the vert ramp is "closed
indefinitely" (rumor has it it is being torn down and a few old guys who skate it
regularly have agreed to "dispose of it" (in a warehouse no doubt)).

Directions to the Beaverton Skatepark:

Driving: From I-5, take Hwy 26 (aka Sunset) westbound (ocean beaches) to the
Cornell/Bethany Rd. exit. Go south, over 26, and left at the t-junction. The third
light is 158th ave, go south (right) and keep your eyes popped for the park on
the left. Tualatin Hills Athletic Center, 503-645-6498.

Transit: Max towards Hillsboro, get off at Merlo/SW 158, take the 67 bus " Jen-
kins-158th to PCC Rock Creek" and you'll see the Tualatin Hills Athletic Center
on the Right and Fred Meyer on the left. The skatepark is on the north side of
the rec center, visible from the road.

The only other gem of a park that is somewhat accessible by Tri-Met is West
Linn. It is about hours bus ride and some walking but the park is amazing if
you want to skate bowls and grind some pool coping. If you have access to a
motor vehicle West Linn is a must because it is only half an hour away.

Directions to the West Linn Skatepark:

Driving: South on I-205, exit #6 -10th St/West Linn go north then east on S.
Salamo Rd uphill. On your right there will be a Safeway/shopping center, go
right on Parker Rd. - the first right after the Safeway. The park is at the bottom
of the hill on the right, park in the lot.

Transit: There is no "easy way" to the park via trimet. The route that went up S.
Salamo got cut so you can get as close as the corner of 10th and Salamo, which
puts you way short and a big hill away. Take the #33-McLaughlin (frequent service line) south from downtown to the Oregon City Transit Center, then transfer
to the #154-Willamette and get off at 10th and Salamo in West Linn. (Please
note: the 154 bus only runs during the day on weekdays.)

If you have access to a car Newberg is a must. Newberg has been called the
"best skatepark in the world" by more than one person, plus Newberg is the
birthplace of Herbert Hoover. The park is 28,000sq.ft. of perfectly poured concrete. It must be experienced to be believed. The park ranges in size from 3'-12'
and features a great vert capsule/elbow combo, snake runs, and more lines that
one person could ever skate. The only thing you need is a helmet and the rule is
actually enforced. The park has shady picnic tables, water fountains and porta-
pottys. Down behind the park (behind the vert section) is a river that makes for

a good place to cool off in the summer. The park is open from sunrise to dark. If youíre into backyard style pools and you've made it to Newberg you should then head to Donald to skate the pool there, complete with steps in the shallow end. For more parks and a complete list of what is available in Oregon to skate visit www.skateoregon.com. this site is the best resource for skating in Oregon, youíll

(eb)

find photos, and directions to more parks than you could skate in a month.

Directions to the Newberg Park:

Head south from Portland on Oregon Route 99W (it's Barbur Blvd out of downtown), when 99W turns into a one way street in downtown Newberg look for Blaine St. (train tracks down the middle) Take a left (south) on Blaine St. all the way (gravel road) to park.

If you skate and are coming into the state from the south via I-5 or 101 I would encourage you to find a layover day in southern Oregon to sample all the parks down south. On I-5 from Ashland to Medford there are great parks and on the coast from Brookings to Astoria there are world class parks. The coast has a world class park about every hour by car--Brookings, Port Orford, Florence, Reedsport, Newport, Lincoln City (X2) and Astoria. Driving in from the east via I-84 the new Milton Freewater park looks to be quite fun and the clover bowl at Hood River is a good time despite being big and scary--at least it is in the shade! There are a number of parks in the Seattle area to sample if you coming from the north (www.sleestak.net) has all the info youíd need on the Washington scene.

www.departmentofskateboarding.com
www.skateoregon.com
www.sleestak.net

Unofficial Play Guide to Portland

If you have children, or occasionally act like one yourself, here's a listing of various kid-friendly stuff in the Rose City:

Water Parks

Common Ground / Inner City Hotsprings- *2927 NE Everett Street 503-238-4010* Has a human-made stream running through their property suitable for rock rummaging and hand splashing. Be unobtrusive and they'll never know you're not waiting for a massage.

Ten Thousand Villages in the Pearl- *914 NW Everett St*

(503) 231-8832 Behind this there is a water sculpture garden with several large fountains and pools, also good for the occasional play.

Jamison Square- *810 NW 11 Ave (at Johnson)* Just don't admit you're from the Eastside and you'll be OK.

Esther Short Park in downtown Vancouver- *W Columbia St. and 8th St.Vancouver, WA* Who knew the Couv could be a destination play place? Still, the water feature in their downtown park is second to none--an urban river.

Grant Park-*NE 33 & U.S. Grant Place* Has the famous Ramona and Ribsy sculpture that splashes water as well as a wading pool that gets filled up on summer days. One great thing about this park is that it is well shaded, unlike Jamison Square.

Play Areas

People's Food Co-op has a great little play nook with toys and books.
3029 SE 21st. Ave (at Tibbets), open daily 9a-9p

Alberta Food Co-op also has a play corner with a very cool custom-built play counter that has cabinets, holes to drop things through, and a toilet flusher. They also have many toys and books. *1500 NE Alberta ST*

The Airport. *Take the MAX Red Line to the Airport.* We are heartbroken that they took away the airplane-themed play area. Were they worried about kids hijacking the play plane? They did replace it with some play equipment, but it's nowhere as cool as being able to radio the plane from the control tower.

Rejuvenation. *1100 SE Grand Avenue - 503-238-1900* OK, so you can't afford to shop here, but there is a great little "play pit" in the downstairs part of the showroom. It's a carpeted, sunken area complete with stairs that only a kid can fit down and lots of toys. There's also a café on the premises.

Kennedy School Hot Tub. *5736 NE 33rd Ave. - 503-249-3983* For $2 and the surrender of your driver's license you and your little ones can use the best hot tub around for as long as you like. It's a great thing to do on a cold, winter day.

East Bank Esplanade. *Along the eastside of the Willamette River from Steel to Hawthorne Bridges* Has cool imported rock formations good for climbing and scrambling. An easy walk from OMSI. Great views of downtown.

Central Library. *801 SW 10th Ave. - 503.988.5123* Has a cool kid's library room with a play house and that amazing tree sculpture.

Awesome Used Clothes for Kids

Children's Clothing Exchange- *3121 SE Division St - 503-230-9621* Run by an awesome couple and their little boy, Justice. Bring stuff and get credit.

Village Merchants. *(503) 234-6343 - 3360 SE Division St* This is the all-purpose stop for household goods, clothes, toys, etc. They have great stuff and decent prices. You can bring stuff and get credit.

Piccolina- *2700 SE 26th Ave - 503-963-8548* Slightly higher prices, but good stuff.

Milagros- *5429 NE 30th Ave - 503-493-4141* New to the neighborhood. Has nice stuff.

Wild Child. *1439 NE Alberta St - 503-249-1030* They have cool hand-made stuff.

Indoor Play

Kennedy School. *5736 NE 33rd Ave. - 503-249-3983* Attachment Parenting Group. Thursday 10-1:00 Free. Community Room

Dishman and Montavilla Community Centers have indoor play parks for 50 cents. They also have scheduled toddler classes.

Matt Dishman Community Center *77 NE Knott - 503-823-3673*

Montavilla Community Center *8219 NE Glisan - 503-823-4101*

Restaurants

Old Wive's Tales. *1300 E Burnside St - 503-238-0470* The original kid-friendly restaurant in town. Has a separate play room. Somewhat expensive, but can be worth it.

Peanut Butter and Ellie's. *1325 NE Fremont St - 503-282-1783* A kid-centric café with chalk boards, magnet boards, lots of toys and books.

The Laurelwood Pub has a small play area with a wooden train set and lots of toys. Warning, most of infant and toddler Portland is there to see and be seen on weekend nights and the scene in the play area can be mosh-pit-like. The scene dies by about 8:30 when their customer-base hits bedtime. *1728 NE 40th Ave - 503-282-0622*

The Tin Shed.   They have a great outdoor courtyard where kids can roam.
1438 NE Alberta St - 503-288-6966

Kennedy School Courtyard Restaurant.   5736 NE 33rd Ave. - 503-249-
3983 Eat outdoors on a sunny day and let your little one run around outside. Or
eat inside and chase the little one around the halls, complete with stairs and
ramps.

Ever-nebulous "Other" Category

Benson Bubblers   *all around town* So most cities have public water fountains, but
none other than Portland have Benson Bubblers. The bubblers were started by civic
leader and wealthy guy Simon Benson in the 'teens. Benson was concerned about all the
drunk loggers seen around town, and figured that if there was a reliable, public source of
drinking water to be found it would curb alcoholism. The first bubbler went into place at
SW 5th and Washington in 1912, and by 1917 40 fountains can be found around town.
Presently there are 52 bubblers, most are of the classic four-bowl design, some are only
single bowls. Make sure you take a drink from one when you're thirsty!

Plaid Pantry   *Locations scattered all over the Portland Metro area* Our own local
7-11, but with a much cheesier name. (And nothing there is plaid, either!) You're probably near one right now. Specializes in 99¢ 24-ounce cans of PBR. FYI: they have a "no
chase policy", and if you really need a job, you can probably get one there.

F.A.T.A.S.S. cheerleaders   Around pdx, you never know when you'll run into The Fat
Action Troupe Allstar Spirit Squad, also known as FATASS. They could be shaking their
fat asses, cheering about size acceptance and loving your body in a bar, a park, a party
or a march. The FATASSes need your help fighting The Body War and are ready to lead the
crowd in a chant of Body Revolution, gonna be a brat, stop the persecution, I am proud
to be fat! (kd)

Queen Size Revolution   *P O Box 4926, Portland, OR 97208 / 503-231-4599*
Through workshops, activism, zines, events and other forums, Queen Size Revolution
provides education to the community about the dangers of fatphobia. Queen Size
Revolution also provides support and community for fat people and their allies. Everyone
is welcome to join Queen Size Revolution who wants to fight against fatphobia and
elminate the tyranny of fat oppression. Queen Size Revolution is also available for
workshops and panels.

Mudeye Puppet Company   *bruce@mudeyepuppets.org / 503 805 0291* The Mudeye Puppet Company teaches folks around Portland how to make puppets out of reused
and recycled materials. Bruce Orr, the directer, also does his own shows, including the
hosting of Portland's biannual PuppetGanza. Mudeye is often at street fairs, celebrations
and anything that involves SCRAP.